ACCESS YOUR ONLINE RESOURCES

Diverse Voices in Educational Practice is accompanied by a number of printable online materials, designed to ensure this resource best supports your professional needs

Activate your online resources:

Go to www.routledge.com/cw/speechmark and click on the cover of this book

Click the 'Sign in or Request Access' button and follow the instructions in order to access the resources

DIVERSE VOICES IN EDUCATIONAL PRACTICE

This practical workbook supports teachers seeking to sensitively understand and respond to the opinions and perceptions of critical stakeholders in student learning and development; pupil voice, parent voice, and professional voice are introduced and explored.

A wide range of expert educator and academic contributors ensure that diverse voices are meaningfully understood, with chapters placing an emphasis on minority and traditionally marginalised groups, including SEND, LGBTQIA+, and Global Majority students. The workbook advocates a clear and inclusive ethos and demonstrates how voice work can help to decolonise the curriculum, promote a positive LGBTQIA+ friendly school climate, and value pupil involvement. Moments for personal reflection, activities, and action plans allow practitioners to consider the role they play in facilitating the effective inclusion of those not normally involved in knowledge construction and decision-making processes.

Blending key theory with practical strategies and takeaways, this workbook is an essential tool for practising primary and secondary teachers and teaching assistants, as well as educational psychologists, school counsellors, and other educational professionals interested in promoting inclusive voice practices.

Alexandra Sewell (she/her) is a Health and Care Professions Council (HCPC) registered educational psychologist and senior lecturer in special educational needs, disability, and inclusion at the University of Worcester. Her research has been published in numerous international journals and explores the concepts of voice and inclusion in education, with a particular interest in student voice in higher education. She is also co-editor of the *International Journal of Birth and Parent Education*.

DIVERSE VOICES IN EDUCATIONAL PRACTICE

A WORKBOOK FOR PROMOTING PUPIL, PARENT AND PROFESSIONAL VOICE

Edited by Alexandra Sewell

Routledge
Taylor & Francis Group

LONDON AND NEW YORK

Cover image: © Getty Images

First published 2023
by Routledge
4 Park Square, Milton Park, Abingdon, Oxon OX14 4RN

and by Routledge
605 Third Avenue, New York, NY 10158

Routledge is an imprint of the Taylor & Francis Group, an informa business

British Library Cataloguing-in-Publication Data
A catalogue record for this book is available from the British Library

Library of Congress Cataloging-in-Publication Data
Diverse voices in educational practice: a workbook for promoting
pupil, parent and professional voice/edited by Alexandra Sewell.
Description: Abingdon, Oxon; New York, NY: Routledge, 2023. |
Includes bibliographical references and index. |
Identifiers: LCCN 2022021335 (print) | LCCN 2022021336 (ebook) | ISBN 9780367761837 (hardcover) |
ISBN 9780367761820 (paperback) | ISBN 9781003165842 (ebook)
Subjects: LCSH: Inclusive education. | Students with disabilities. | Sexual minority students. |
School environment–Social aspects.
Classification: LCC LC1200 .D58 2023 (print) | LCC LC1200 (ebook) |
DDC 371.82–dc23/eng/20220706
LC record available at https://lccn.loc.gov/2022021335
LC ebook record available at https://lccn.loc.gov/2022021336

ISBN: 978-0-367-76183-7 (hbk)
ISBN: 978-0-367-76182-0 (pbk)
ISBN: 978-1-003-16584-2 (ebk)

DOI: 10.4324/9781003165842

Typeset in Din
by Deanta Global Publishing Services, Chennai, India

Access the companion website: www.routledge.com/cw/speechmark

To Jonas Brown.
May you find your voice and never lose it.

CONTENTS

Contents

ACKNOWLEDGEMENTS

My sincerest thanks go to the contributors who kindly shared their expertise and experiences for this book.

Thank you to my husband for proofreading each chapter and encouraging me through the daunting task of writing and editing whilst we became parents during a global pandemic.

Thank you to my editor at Speechmark, Clare Ashworth, for being passionate about the concept and understanding when the final manuscript took a little while longer to emerge than planned.

CONTRIBUTORS

Alexandra Baird (she/her)

Alexandra Baird was raised by parents who allowed her the freedom to find her own path. She came out to her dad at 21 after her first relationship break-up, but it took another 15 years before she was truly authentic at work. Her wife, Jen, and pet dog Coco, a black/tan miniature dachshund, are her absolute world.

Naomi Boswell (she/her)

Naomi Boswell is an educational and child psychologist within a local authority in North West England. Her professional interests include autism spectrum condition and promoting participation and co-production with young people in practice. Naomi is also an honorary tutor at the University of Manchester. Twitter: @Naomilouiset.

Stuart Busby (he/him)

Stuart Busby has been a successful UK schools' leader for 20 years and is currently leading improvement across a range of settings. He developed sustained educational partnerships with schools in Europe and Tanzania. As part of this work, he has earned a distinction in a Masters in Educational Leadership and is currently pursuing a PhD exploring the impact of head teacher training in the Tanga region of Tanzania. Twitter: @busby_stuart.

Max Davies (they/them)

Max Davies is a newly appointed doctorate student at the University of Brighton. Their research interests are gender creative parenting and children raised with they/them pronouns from birth. This includes the discourse of gender in children, predominantly in the early years. Max has passion and personal interest within this subject area which directs and navigates their work.

Erica Douglas-Osborn (no preference)

Erica Douglas-Osborn is a senior specialist child and educational psychologist within a local authority in Greater Manchester. She has a keen interest in developing systems to support children and young people to be able to advocate for themselves. Erica is also an honorary tutor at Manchester University and published author.

Hannah Fleming (she/her)

Hannah Fleming is an educational psychologist in the South West. She is a consultant educational psychologist to a specialist school for children with social communication needs and is the local authority educational psychologist for the virtual school, working with schools to support young people who have a social worker. Twitter: @hannah_edpsych

Rachel Helme (she/her)

Having worked as a secondary school mathematics teacher for ten years, Rachel Helme is currently completing her PhD at the University of Bristol. Her research interests are mathematical identity work in the context of the low attainment label and developing poetic inquiry research methods. Twitter: @HelmeRachel

Angela Hodgkins (she/her)

Angela Hodgkins is a senior lecturer at the University of Worcester. Angela had a varied career working with children and families for over 20 years before moving to the University of Worcester, where she is a Course Leader. She is also a qualified counsellor and is currently working towards a PhD on empathy within the early years. Twitter: @a_hodgkins

Anastasia Kennett (she/her)

Anastasia Kennett is a PhD student and associate lecturer at the University of Worcester in the School of Education. Anastasia has undertaken research projects exploring student voice in collaboration with Alexandra Sewell. Her most recent PhD research explores student voice with students with diverse learner needs in higher education.

Janchai King (she/her)

Janchai King is a senior practitioner educational psychologist working in an educational psychology team in London and as an academic and professional tutor at the Tavistock and Portman NHS Foundation Trust. She is particularly interested in working in collaborative and meaningful ways with young people engaging with youth justice services.

Max Kirk (they/them)

Max Kirk is a 23-year trans, queer individual. Their first degree was an integrated masters in maths and chemistry, but they have sidestepped into the social sciences. They are currently doing an MRes in social research methods, as part of a White Rose 1+3 doctoral studentship. They start their PhD this coming autumn, 2022. Their research interests centre on trans (and LGBTQIA+) youth within formal and informal education. Outside of their studies, they do a lot of voluntary youth work and love to read queer/trans fiction.

Klaudia Matasovska (she/her)

Klaudia Matasovska is a special educational needs educator and a PhD student in the Department of Educational Studies at Goldsmiths, University of London. Her research interests are centred on the educational system's ways of addressing LGBTQIA+ inclusion with regard to pupils with special educational needs and disabilities (SEND). Prior to her PhD studies, she held a leadership position managing the behaviour and attitudes area in a SEND school in London.

Jane Park (she/her)

Jane Park is a specialist practitioner educational psychologist in the West Midlands. Her publications include a chapter in the British Psychological Society's book *Applied Educational Psychology With 16–25 Year Olds*, a paper on the transition experiences of autistic young adults, and a contribution to a forthcoming EPASIG book. Twitter: @viola_jane

Kara Pirttijarvi (she/her)

Kara Pirttijarvi is a trainee educational psychologist in her final year of studying for a professional doctorate in educational and child psychology (University of East London). Kara graduated in psychology (Goldsmiths), and has completed a Postgraduate Certificate of Education (Institute of Education) and an MSc in genetics, environment and development in psychology and psychiatry (King's College). Her passions include exploring emotional processes in learning and supporting self-advocacy in young people with additional needs.

Maninder Kaur Sangar (she/her)

Maninder Kaur Sangar is an educational psychologist working within a local authority in the West Midlands. Maninder is interested in critical psychological approaches which enable taken-for-granted practices to be deconstructed and marginalised voices to be heard.

Pippa Sterk (they/she)

Pippa Sterk is a second-year PhD candidate in the School of Education, Communication and Society at King's College London, where they also teach on the BA Social Sciences. Their research explores the experiences of LGBTQIA+ volunteers in higher education. Twitter: @PippaSterk.

Jennifer Zwarthoed (she/her)

Jennifer Zwarthoed is a PhD researcher at the University of Portsmouth. With her roots as a secondary health teacher from the Netherlands, she has experience in teaching sexual education in both Austria and the Netherlands. Her current research focuses on the inclusion of LGBTQIA+ identities in sex education practices.

Chapter 1

INTRODUCTION

Voice, Power, and Action in Schools

Alexandra Sewell

Introduction

This chapter will:

- Describe the conception and rationale of the text.
- Outline what is meant by voice, power, and social justice, as these are foundational concepts for growing your own voice practice.
- Introduce the concept of meaningful voice practice and enable you to develop your own personal definition.

Introduction to text
Aim

The aim of this workbook is to support busy education professionals to understand the importance and impact of voice practices and to be inspired to develop their own. It is hoped that readers will wish to orient towards a social justice stance by seeking new ways to meaningfully canvass, understand, and act upon the views, perceptions, and opinions of a wide range of stakeholders in education.

How to read this book

It is likely that you come to the content of this book already possessing an interest in working collaboratively with others in a supportive way. You may have your own positive experience of someone listening closely to your opinions, which has inspired you to do the same. Or you may have had the opposite experience where you know what it is like to not be listened to and are keen to do differently yourself. Either way, the purpose of this book is to enhance this interest by providing you with reflective and practical activities that will enable you to translate key theory into your own educational practice.

DOI: 10.4324/9781003165842-1

Whilst the book can be read cover to cover, it is acknowledged that not all sections shall necessarily be relevant to all people. Whilst it is advisable to start with Chapter 1, as it provides an overview of key theory, each chapter can thereafter be read individually and in any order, based on your own interests and needs. You are fully encouraged to engage with all the workbook activities that draw your attention, as they have been designed to fit into a busy work schedule.

Position statement

In qualitative social science research, a position statement allows the researcher to reveal key aspects of who they are and the context within which they are working in order to address any potential bias (Willig, 2013). I shall write this section in the first person, as the purpose is to position my own experiences and perspective in relation to the content of this book. There are two contextual factors that influenced the creation of this book. Firstly, the tumultuous global events of 2020. Secondly, my own lived experiences with mental ill-health and having my voice either respected or ignored by professionals.

The idea for this book came to me during the summer of 2020. The Covid-19 pandemic had exposed and worsened existing inequalities. More than ever, professionals working in education were cultivating a sense of personal enlightenment towards the perspectives of others, especially towards those from traditionally marginalised groups. I came to believe that a book which combined theory with practical application would be a valuable resource for helping with this important task.

With regard to my own lived experience, it is important to acknowledge my privilege. I am a white, middle-class woman who has had the good fortune to grow up in a stable and economically developed country. I have had ready access to education, and my voice has been listened to and deemed important by the society I live in. For this reason, I sought many collaborations from contributors in the development of this book. It is my hope that a strong sense of allyship is achieved through these collaborations.

As part of my position statement, it is also important to disclose that I have lived experience of significant mental ill-health. Whilst for much of my life I have considered myself as experiencing good mental health, there have been two periods of significant mental ill-health. Once when I experienced generalised anxiety disorder and a psychotic break down, and a second after an experience of birth trauma and related post-traumatic stress disorder, where I spent time as an inpatient in a psychiatric hospital. It is my interactions with both wonderful professionals, especially in the hospital setting, who have championed my voice, and the rare but influential experience of those who have not validated my perspective that have strongly influenced my desire to author this book and the shaping of its contents.

Reflective activity

Write your own position statement with regard to engaging in voice practice in education. Consider your own background and experiences as well as the wider educational and cultural context you work within.

My position statement:

_____

_____

_____

_____

Figure 1.1

Growing your voice practice

The aim of this workbook is to help you grow your own voice practice as an educational practitioner. By this I mean that you will be able to canvass, interpret, and respond to the opinions and perceptions of a wide range of stakeholders involved in the education of a child or young person.

In this section you are introduced to four foundational concepts to help you grow your own voice practice. It is helpful to think about each key concept following on from the next when related to the growth of your personal practice. Firstly, what constitutes "voice," and what doesn't, needs to be understood. This is the seed of your practice. Secondly, for a voice practice to begin growing, social justice needs to be adopted as a central value. Thirdly, for a voice practice to grow strong, existing power imbalances need to be recognised and challenged. Finally, for a voice practice to fully bloom, the more abstract, yet deeper, concept of discriminatory epistemic justice needs to be appreciated.

Voice

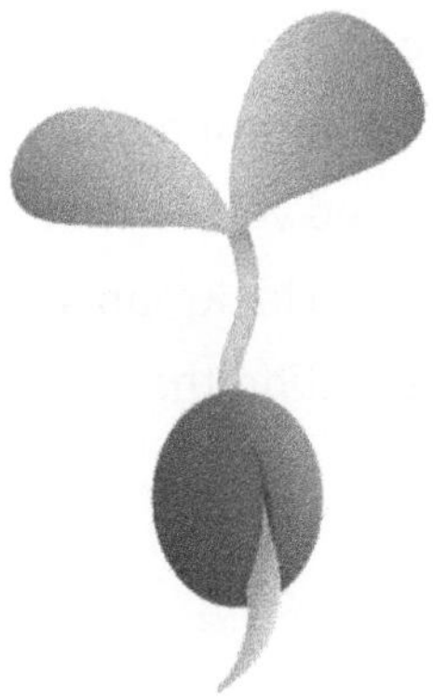

What is meant by the term "voice" can be perplexing. Further still, subsidiary terms such as "student voice," "parental voice," and "voice of the child" all have singular definitions, which are covered in depth in following chapters. It is therefore important to outline what is meant by voice as the seed to any educator's professional practice.

When we think of voice, the first idea that springs to mind is most likely that of language spoken out loud. We may then perhaps consider written language. This is an oversimplistic and non-inclusive

Figure 1.2

definition of voice. When used in an educational context, voice primarily encompasses an individual's, or group of individuals', unique views, opinions, and perspectives. It is understood to be rooted within their own frames of reference, developed through personal experience. It is also equally resultant of the wider cultures and cultural norms the protagonist(s) may act within.

Voice can be expressed via many different mediums and means. A person does not have to rely on language alone to have a voice and be able to express it. The job of an educator is to find ways to adapt to everyone and their circumstances so that their opinions and perspectives are given due weight and value.

Social justice

Figure 1.3

The concept of social justice has arguably fallen into the trap of multiple definitions and theorisation, allowing it to be critiqued for being ambiguous and lacking in meaning (Cochran-Smith, Shakman, Jong, Terrell, Barnatt, & McQuillan, 2009). Hackman (2005, p. 104), however, offers a clear definition for the application of social justice within an educational context:

Social justice ... does not merely examine difference or diversity but pays careful attention to the systems of power and privilege that give rise to social inequality, and encourages students to critically examine oppression on institutional, cultural, and individual levels in search of opportunities for social action in the service of social change.

This definition has been chosen from the many available, as it is helps us to see how voice practice can be impactful in real-world contexts. When this definition is adopted, the goal of voice practices is framed as being to challenge systems of power and privilege by creating space for the involvement of those who traditionally haven't been involved with or impacted on educational processes. It is hoped that through this inclusion of marginalised voices that social inequality can be challenged. Voice practice is therefore closely linked to Hackman's definition of social justice, as it can be viewed as a form of progressive social action that can influence powerful social change.

Power

If power and systems of power are to be challenged by practitioners in education, then in order to grow their voice practice this too needs to be uniquely understood. Like social justice, the notion of power has been conceptualised and applied in many ways with a plethora of theories, far beyond the scope of the current text.

A direct and applicable understanding is best for busy educational professionals seeking to develop their voice practice whilst coping with the realities of the job. Power exists in all social contexts and is incredibly influential in how we interact with each other. Those who have power hold it by varying degrees, which will be different in

Figure 1.4

every situation and in flux over time and place. Fundamentally, those who have more influence and say are those in the position of holding power, and those who have less influence and say are those in the position of holding less or no power. Those with power are privileged in that they have more impact in the shaping and directing of educational contexts and practices.

Although there are obvious positions of power and existing power structures in education, such as a head teacher having power and control over the running of a school, there are also more subtle power dynamics. When considering how power may be influencing voice and voice practices in your own educational context, observing and responding to obvious power structures is a good place to start. However, do not be afraid to critically analyse any nuanced power dynamics which appear once a critical, social justice orientation is adopted.

Discriminatory epistemic injustice

Examples of social injustice are, for the most part, demonstrable in a tangible, real-world way. For example, if a person from a minority background is a suitable job candidate but is not interviewed, it is likely that discrimination may well have been at play. However, the concept of discriminatory epistemic injustice shows us that injustice also occurs at the epistemic level.

Epistemology is the philosophical study of knowledge and what we deem to be true. Epistemic injustice is one way of describing injustices that occur when certain groups are excluded from societies' creation of what is deemed to be right, factual, and true. It also occurs because certain groups are left out of important cultural

Figure 1.5

discussions because they do not have access to the same information or an understanding of shared linguistic practices (Kidd, Medina, & Pohlaus, 2019).

Fricker (2007, 2017) outlined two types of discriminatory epistemic injustice. Testimonial injustice occurs when a listener discredits a communicator's information because of a prior-held prejudice about them or a social group they are perceived to belong to. For example, a teacher may ignore a teaching assistant who belongs to a minority group who shares information about a child's progress, as the teacher holds prior prejudices that members of that group are untrustworthy and irrational. Because of their existing prejudice, they do not believe that the teaching assistant is credible and that the information they share is trustworthy.

The second is hermeneutical injustice, which occurs because a listener cannot understand the knowledge that is being spoken to them, as they do not share the same concepts as the speaker or group of speakers. For example, a teaching assistant new to the field of education may try their best to understand what a teacher is telling them about how they teach but may not understand educational concepts and acronyms used in the explanation. In this way, the teaching assistant is experiencing an injustice, as due to lack of understanding they cannot equally participate by putting forward their own ideas.

Both types of discriminatory epistemic injustice are important to understand, as voice practice is an epistemic activity. To seek to develop your voice practice is to seek knowledge and views on "truth" from others who have a different perspective to you, and therefore construct a different understanding of the shared social reality. We must consider if any prior prejudice towards a speaker means we are discrediting their information (testimonial injustice). Or if we are using language that may exclude a person from understanding what we really mean and, in turn, explaining themselves (hermeneutical injustice). This is why discriminatory epistemic injustice is placed as the final concept to grasp; it is only when we accept the personal epistemic life another shares, whilst holding our own prejudices in mind, that voice practices truly bloom (Sewell, 2016).

Reflective activity

In this section you have been introduced to four foundational concepts for growing your voice practice:

- Voice.

- Social justice.

- Power.

- Discriminatory epistemic injustice.

This reflective activity will help you consolidate your learning and begin to develop your own thoughts and opinions regarding these concepts. In each of the four quadrants in Figure 1.6 there is space to jot down your first ideas that spring to mind after having read each section. You don't need to take copious notes. Aim to spend a few minutes on each quadrant. Experiment with using a selection of single words, pictures, and short sentences. Focus on the key differences between each concept. How do they relate, but how are they unique?

Voice	Social Justice
Power	Discriminatory Epistemic Injustice

Figure 1.6

Meaningful voice practice

In this section you will develop a personal understanding of the concept of meaningful voice practice. The concept can be deceptively simple; voice practices can only be meaningful if they result in tangible action that directly address power imbalances as an act of social justice promotion. To develop your own thinking regarding meaningful voice practice, selected theories and reflection activities are presented. After working through these you will have the opportunity to produce your own definition of meaningful voice practice.

Arnstein's ladder of citizen participation (1969)

It is hard to argue against a moral idea; to put it into practice is a significant task. Sherry Arnstein said this of meaningful voice practice, stating that it is "a little bit like eating spinach; no one is against it in principle because it is good for you" (1969, p. 216). We can all agree that eating spinach and meaningful voice practice are both good, in principle, but to engage in them in reality is harder to accomplish.

The have-nots

Arnstein's (1969) ladder of citizen participation is a seminal model of citizen participation. Sixty years later its central ideas continue to influence educational professionals who seek to engage with and act on the voices and perspectives of others. The first concept to understand is Arnstein's idea that in any context where power is at play there are those who are the "haves" and those who are the "have-nots." To be a have-not is to be traditionally and systematically removed from, and not granted access to, decision-making processes. For example, having an influence in what is deemed important information, how information is shared, what goals are set, and any related structural changes to practice and policy.

Reflective activity

To explore this idea further, consider a context in which you work, such as a school or local educational authority. Use the headings in Figure 1.7 to briefly mind-map who you think are the haves and who are the have-nots. Are you surprised by any of your ideas? Why do you think you are surprised, and what may this be telling you about who traditionally doesn't have power (have-nots) and why within this context?

Citizen participation is citizen power

Arguably, the biggest influence in the development of the model was the critique that citizen participation can be used by professionals as a buzz word. This means that professionals claim that they are including the opinions and ideas of the have-nots in a democratic way, but in practice this does not result in any actual influence. Such voice practices are implemented for show. Arnstein (1969, p. 216) poignantly described this as an "empty ritual of participation."

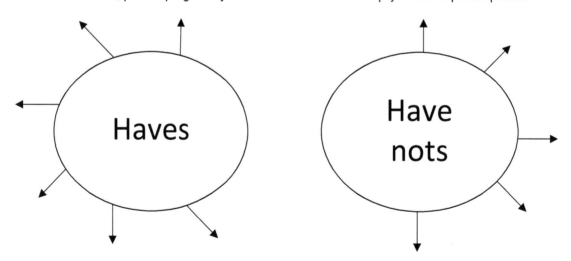

Figure 1.7

Citizen participation can be said to have occurred if there has been a true redistribution of power. This can only be achieved if the act of involving have-nots leads to them implementing true change. As such, citizen participation *is* citizen power. If no change occurs, then it is just paying lip service to the *idea* of citizen participation. It is this notion that is referred to specifically throughout the book when the concept of *meaningful voice practice* is continually explored.

Reflective activity

Can you think of a time someone appeared to be listening to your perspectives and opinions, but it didn't result in any tangible, meaningful change? What did that experience feel like? It is likely that you agree with Arnstein who claimed that such meaningless forms of engagement leave people feeling frustrated.

Types of participation and non-participation

Based on these concepts and ideas, Arnstein developed the ladder of citizen participation as a typology of citizen power/engagement. There are eight levels of participation. Those at the bottom rungs of the ladder reflect less meaningful, more for-show types of participation. Those at the higher rungs of the ladder demonstrate meaningful forms of participation as citizen power is truly occurring.

1. Manipulation: At the first level, from the bottom up, there is no genuine participation. The guise of participation is used to manipulate the have-nots into thinking they have been listened to, to promote the agenda of those in power.

Real-world example: A head teacher calls a team meeting with school staff and tells them about a new plan for teaching arts-based subjects in the school. The plan has already been finalised and teachers are told their signatures are required to support the plan. Teachers initially feel they have a say because they were called to the meeting and asked to support the plan. However, once their signatures are gained, they realise there was much they were not told about the plan. They are expected to blindly follow the plan, as their "support" was said to be sought before implementation, via the signatures.

2. Therapy: At the second level, group therapy is used as an example of how participant involvement can seek to change perceived problems in the have-nots to avoid making meaningful changes to the systems that oppress them.

Real-world example: A group of parents with children with Special Educational Needs and Disabilities (SEND) express a concern to the Local Education Authority (LEA) that their expertise and knowledge is not sufficiently considered by professionals when services are designed to support a pupil's social, emotional, and behavioural needs. Instead of responding to this feedback by making changes to its services, the LEA offers all parents who spoke up access to a group parenting course, indicating a belief that they need to become "better" at parenting.

3. Informing: Level three of the ladder is acknowledged as the first step towards legitimate citizen involvement, as information is shared without deliberate attempts at manipulation. However, information only flows from the haves to the have-nots, with limited opportunity for feedback.

Real-world example: A school's pastoral lead wishes to alert parents about changes to their safeguarding policy, so they create and distribute a leaflet on the topic. By the time parents respond with queries and ideas the policy has already been finalised and implemented.

4. Consultation: At level four, there is an attempt to canvass opinions, often through surveys and public hearings. However, this data is mostly obtained to show that views were canvassed, but they are rarely acted on.

Real-world example: A department head in a secondary school creates a survey to collect the opinions of teachers in the department regarding how it is run. The department head selects the topic of the questions to reflect their own concerns about the department, limiting the scope of participant answers. These are the concerns that get passed on to senior management.

5. Placation: At level five of the ladder, citizens begin to be more actively involved with some emerging influence, but tokenism still exists in different forms. Whilst the have-nots may be involved in development processes, those in traditional power still hold the majority influence and make all final decisions. The rights of citizens and their involvement are poorly defined.

Real-world example: A school starts a school council but strategically selects which children will sit on the council. Children who are "most able" and biddable to adult demands are chosen to monitor and control pupil involvement in school issues. As such, the views of other children are missed in the process, and the pupils involved are not entirely sure about their rights and the impact they could have.

6. Partnership: At level six of the ladder, power begins to be redistributed between power holders and have-nots via their involvement in shared planning processes such as the development of advisory boards. Citizens should also be given adequate education and access to resources to meaningfully understand existing processes, language, and structures.

Real-world example: A school develops a parent advisory board. Parents first receive training on existing school processes, educational legislation, and terminology so they are fully educated on existing systems and the influence they could have to change them. The committee is given an adequate monetary budget to implement their ideas. This budget is routinely re-evaluated and adjusted considering parent's ideas and initiatives.

7. Delegated power: At level seven, the have-nots are given true decision-making authority over a particular issue and initiative. For this to be meaningful, the have-nots must have a majority share in decision-making processes, with traditional power holders being the ones in the bargaining position.

Real-world example: A class teacher allows students to use Friday afternoons to choose the curriculum they would like to study and the activities they would like to engage with. The class puts forward ideas and all students vote on the final chosen one. The teacher does not intervene or direct by offering ideas or shaping proposed ideas. If the teacher wants to have more of a say, they must ask the class directly, as the final decision is democratically chosen by all children.

8. Citizen power: At the final level of the ladder, true citizen participation occurs when the have-nots gain full charge of policy and managerial elements. Though once viewed as outsiders, they are now in a position of meaningful power to be able to negotiate and make substantial changes.

Real-world example: Arguably, citizen power will not be fully achieved until marginalised and majority groups are proportionally represented across all aspects of the education system. This means they are fulfilling positions of senior leadership, headship, and beyond. The prospective reality of this is explored in depth in subsequent chapters.

Reflective activity

The following activity is designed to help you apply the ladder of citizen participation to your own practice. Consider this a note-taking and in-the-moment reflective activity that can easily slot into your working day.

Keep the table in Figure 1.8 on hand somewhere that can be easily accessed throughout your workday. Every time you recognise an action or behaviour that is intended to gain the opinions, ideas, and perspectives of others, jot it down and place it on whichever rung of the ladder of citizen participation you think it may be occurring within, with some brief notes as to why. You can refer to the real-world examples to help you.

Over time you will be able to map several elements of practice across the ladder. This will give you a visual representation of citizen participation within the context you are working in. This is a good starting point for self-evaluating your own practice but could also be used to evaluate the practice of a group or whole system.

Ladder of Participation		Daily notes and reflections on voice practice
Degrees of citizen power	Citizen control	
	Delegated power	
	Partnership	
Degrees of tokenism	Placation	
	Consultation	
	Informing	
Non - participation	Therapy	
	Manipulation	
SUMMARY NOTES:		

Figure 1.8

Tokenism

Tokenism is an important concept in meaningful voice work. It has been broadly defined as have-nots being listened to but not being equally involved or exerting equal influence in decision-making processes (Lundy, 2007). Lundy (2018) argues that the risk of tokenistic voice practices can lead professionals to avoid canvassing the opinions and perceptions of those they represent. It is assumed by practitioners that it is better to avoid voice work altogether than to engage in it in a tokenistic way.

However, tokenistic voice practices can also be seen as a stepping stone to more meaningful voice practices (Lundy, 2018). Although not the ideal way to engage in exploring the perceptions of others in education, tokenistic voice practice may lead to meaningful engagement in the long run and can help develop the skills of both participants and those in power seeking the perceptions of others. As such, when engaging in the activities in this book do not feel deflated if your existing or initial voice practice appears to be tokenistic. Instead, try to see this as a starting point – a well-intentioned initial attempt that can be developed and deepened, a transitionary stage.

Behavioural integrity: Espoused versus enacted values
Word–deed alignment

The concept of behavioural integrity is also concerned with the importance of direct action. In this case, the relationship of leaders' and employees' actions to an organisation's values. There are many definitions of what values consist of, but they are commonly agreed to be a set of beliefs that endure over a significant period, that direct socially desirable behaviour, and are meta-contextual rather than being significant to a specific situation (Rokeach, 1973; Schwartz, 2012).

Espoused values are values important for institutional culture and employee behaviour that leaders state publicly as being key to the running of the organisation (Gopinath, Nair, & Thangaraj, 2018). Organisations like schools or the LEA directly state their espoused values in a range of formal ways, such as vision and mission statements, policy documents, formal aims, slogans and mottoes, and in day-to-day discourse (Gopinath et al., 2018). For example, a school may have the motto "Achievement for All," which espouses the values of inclusion and success.

Enacted values are those which are implemented in action by the leaders and staff of an organisation (Gopinath et al., 2018; Simons, Tomlinson, & Leroy, 2011). There is a risk that enacted values are not congruent with espoused values. Incongruence can emerge through how a school conducts its business and how it treats is employees, pupils, and parents (Gopinath et al., 2018). This occurs through day-to-day actions. It is this importance of word–deed alignment that is implicated in behavioural integrity (Simons, 2002). To put it colloquially, are school staff doing what they say they do with regard to their values? If they are not, then their espoused values do not align with their enacted values and they are not achieving behavioural integrity (Simons et al., 2011). Conversely, if their day-to-day behaviours are reflective of their espoused values, then behavioural integrity is achieved.

Implications for meaningful voice practice

Behavioural integrity is a less complex concept than power and social justice, as it is simply concerned with the alignment of daily work behaviours to espoused values (Simons et al., 2011). This provides a good starting place for educational practitioners wishing to reflect on the meaningfulness of their own voice practices. Are you espousing the value of listening to the voice of others? If so, to what extent are your daily work behaviours, and those of others in your educational context, aligning with this espoused value?

Behavioural integrity has been shown to influence the development of trust between stakeholders in an organisation (Engelbrecht, Heine, & Mahembe, 2017; Kistan, 2019). The more consistently school leaders and school staff align their enacted values and espoused values, the more they show behavioural reliability, which over time leads observers to interpret them as trustworthy (Engelbrecht et al., 2017; Kistan, 2019). Behavioural reliability can be a clearly actionable route to meaningful voice practice, as for it to occur, staff behaviours consistently need to reflect the value of representing and responding to the perceptions and views of others. The presence of behavioural integrity in a setting also correlates with employee's commitment to the institution, job satisfaction, positive affect towards the organisation, and identification with leaders (Davis & Rothstein, 2006).

Reflective activity

This activity gives you the opportunity to consider whether behavioural integrity is present in your current educational setting (see Figure 1.9). The activity can be used flexibly; you could consider the professional behaviour of senior leadership, all team members, your own behaviour, or a combination of all of these. First, consult all documents you have access to that espouse the organisation's values regarding voice practices, power, and social justice,

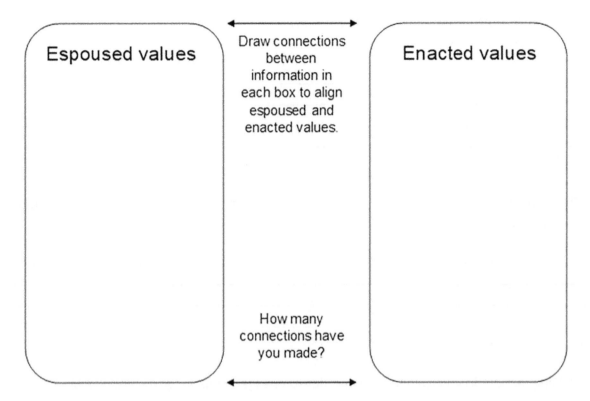

Figure 1.9

and make a note of these in the space titled "Espoused values." Use the second space titled "Enacted values" to note actual behaviours. Use the questions to compare the information you have placed in the two boxes and consider to what extent you think behavioural integrity is present.

Conclusion: Your personal definition of meaningful voice practice

At the start of this section, meaningful voice practice was defined as tangible action based on the views, opinions, and perceptions of key stakeholders which directly address power imbalances as an act of social justice promotion. Seemingly a simple definition, the selected exploration of Arnstein's ladder of citizen participation, the work of Lundy (2018), and the concept of behavioural integrity was made to enable you to explore this in more depth. You have used each theory as a lens to reflect on your own professional experiences and perceptions. The final task for this section is to develop your own personal definition of meaningful voice practice. Write your own conceptual statement for "meaningful voice practice" using the questions in Figure 1.10 as a guide

Q1: What is most important to you as an educational practitioner when seeking to listen to and understand the views and opinions of others?

_____

_____

_____

_____

Q2: What do you think 'power' is and how important is it in your definition of meaningful voice practice?

_____

_____

_____

_____

Q3: What action do you wish to take in order to engage in meaningful voice practice?

_____

_____

_____

_____

My personal definition of meaningful voice practice:

_____

_____

_____

_____

Figure 1.10

Chapter summary

The purpose of this workbook is to inspire educational professionals to engage in meaningful voice practice. What is meant by meaningful voice practice builds on key theories of Arnstein's ladder of citizen participation, tokenism (Lundy, 2018), and behavioural integrity (Engelbrecht et al., 2017; Kistan, 2019). Essentially, voice practice should not only canvass the opinions and perceptions of others in an appropriate way, but should also lead to specific and purposeful action and change closely related to those opinions and perceptions. The concepts of voice, social justice, power, and epistemic injustice have been presented as foundational constructs to understand when beginning to develop one's own voice practice.

The following chapters expand on these concepts by applying them to develop meaningful voice practice for a range of stakeholders in education. You will find yourself returning to the activities you have engaged with here to reflect again on your first thoughts. Please do so – promoting the voice of others is a dramatic act of inclusion that requires personal dedication based on your own values and passion for equality, social justice, and fairness.

Further reading

Epistemic Injustice by Miranda Fricker – This comprehensive text presents a deep exploration of the concept of epistemic injustice. Whilst certainly not a quick read, perseverance will be rewarded, as it provides a full discussion of the topic.

Power and Education: Contexts of Oppression and Opportunity by Antonia Kupfer – As acknowledged in this chapter, power is a complex phenomenon which influences educational practice in a myriad of ways. This comprehensive text is a good starting point for those interested in exploring further.

References

Arnstein, S. R. (1969). A ladder of citizen participation. *Journal of the American Institute of Planners*, *35*(4), 216–224.

Cochran-Smith, M., Shakman, K., Jong, C., Terrell, D. G., Barnatt, J., & McQuillan, P. (2009). Good and just teaching: The case for social justice in teacher education. *American Journal of Education*, *115*(3), 347–377.

Davis, A. L., & Rothstein, H. R. (2006). The effects of the perceived behavioral integrity of managers on employee attitudes: A meta-analysis. *Journal of Business Ethics*, *67*(4), 407–419.

Engelbrecht, A. S., Heine, G., & Mahembe, B. (2017). Integrity, ethical leadership, trust and work engagement. *Leadership & Organization Development Journal*, *38*(3), 368–379.

Fricker, M. (2007). *Epistemic injustice: The power and ethics of knowing.* Oxford: Oxford University Press.

Fricker, M. (2017). Evolving concepts of epistemic injustice. In Kidd, I. J., Medina, J., & Pohlhaus Jr, G., (eds.), *Routledge handbook of epistemic injustice. Routledge handbooks in philosophy* (pp. 53–60) London: Routledge.

Hackman, H. W. (2005). Five essential components for social justice education. *Equity & Excellence in Education*, *38*(2), 103–109.

Kidd, I. J., Medina, J., & Pohlhaus, G. (2019). *The Routledge handbook of epistemic injustice.* London: Routledge.

Kistan, K. (2019). *The relationship amongst behavioural integrity, trust and innovative work behaviour* (Doctoral dissertation, University of Pretoria). Available at: https://repository.up.ac.za/bitstream/handle/2263/68864/Kistan_Relationship_2018.pdf?sequence=1 [Retrieved: 26 October 2020].

Lundy, L. (2007). 'Voice' is not enough: conceptualising Article 12 of the United Nations Convention on the Rights of the Child. *British Educational Research Journal*, *33*(6), 927–942.

Lundy, L. (2018). In defence of tokenism? Implementing children's right to participate in collective decision-making. *Childhood*, *25*(3), 340–354.

Rokeach, M. (1973). *The nature of human values*. New York: Free Press.

Schwartz, S. H. (2012). An overview of the Schwartz theory of basic values. *Online readings in Psychology and Culture*, *2*(1).

Sewell, A. (2016). A theoretical application of epistemological oppression to the psychological assessment of special educational needs; concerns and practical implications for anti-oppressive practice. *Educational Psychology in Practice*, *32*(1), 1–12.

Simons, T. (2002). Behavioral integrity: The perceived alignment between managers' words and deeds as a research focus. *Organization Science*, *13*(1), 18–35.

Simons, T. L., Tomlinson, E. C., & Leroy, H. (2011). Research on behavioral integrity: A promising construct for positive organizational scholarship. [Electronic version]. From Cornell University, School of Hotel Administration: http://scholarship.sha.cornell.edu/articles/894 [Retrieved 26 October 2020].

Willig, C. (2013). *Introducing qualitative research in psychology*. London: McGraw-Hill Education.

Chapter 2

PUPIL VOICE

Listening to, Understanding, and Acting on
Pupil Perceptions and Opinions

*Alexandra Sewell, Naomi Boswell, Erica Douglas-Osborn,
and Rachel Helme*

Introduction

This chapter will:

- Introduce pupil voice by presenting different ways of understanding what pupil voice is and the inclusion of pupil voice in policy and legislation.

- Support you in auditing your own pupil voice practice to develop an action plan.

- Explore co-production as an example of an effective and egalitarian procedure for gathering pupil voice (contributed by Naomi Boswell and Erica Douglas-Osborn).

- Present a case example of listening and responding to an individual student (contributed by Rachel Helme).

What is pupil voice?

Teachers listen to their pupils all day; to teach is to listen. Educators listen in the simplest of ways. Consider the reception class teacher listening patiently to a 5-year-old sharing that last night they had chocolate cake for pudding. Educators also listen in complex and courageous ways. Consider the pastoral lead listening to a teenager share their story of abuse at home. Ultimately, educational professionals listen in a myriad of ways which enhance teaching and learning.

Pupil voice is a concept which tries to capture and formalise the natural tendency teachers and other educational professionals have towards listening to children and young people. It is often used synonymously with the terms "student voice," "learner voice," and "pupil participation" (Fielding, 2009, as cited in Czerniawski, 2012). In this section you will be

DOI: 10.4324/9781003165842-2

introduced to the concept of pupil voice before specific examples of theory and practice are presented in depth in the rest of the chapter. To help deepen your understanding, different conceptualisations and typologies of pupil voice are explored and the rise of the practice will be charted through policy and legislation development.

Personal reflection activities have been created to support your understanding as you explore what pupil voice is. These activities relate to the action plan you are encouraged to develop at the end of the chapter.

Conceptualising pupil voice

Two major narratives have emerged which conceptualise pupil voice in starkly different ways. As such, pupil voice has been viewed as "a flexible term rooted in traditions with opposing educational visions" (Vainker, 2021, p. 26). Fielding (2004a), a leading author in pupil voice, outlined these different perspectives as person centred versus high performance. A person-centred approach sees children and young people as equal partners and aims to create a sense of community. The high-performance narrative views pupil voice as an endeavour that should be undertaken to increase school performance, bettering objective educational outcomes. Similarly, Czerniawski (2010) writes of an "empowerment/democratic education" narrative, keen to involve pupils in a fair and radical way, versus a "policy technology" narrative, where pupil feedback is used to improve the efficiency of the school as an organisation.

Person centred/empowerment

The appeal of a person-centred/empowerment conceptualisation of pupil voice is the belief that recognising pupils have valid perspectives and opinions is humanising and democratising (Hart, 1992; Fielding, 2001; Flutter & Ruddock, 2004). For example, Hart (1992) adapted the ladder of citizen participation (Arnstein, 1969) (see Chapter 1) for use with children to expose them to their citizen rights from a young age, arguing that doing so will enable them to successfully engage in democracy. Similarly, Fielding (2004b) propagated the "students as researchers" agenda where students were involved in school development in a dialogic way that not only listened to them but also allowed them to set the agenda for change. It was argued that this led to a transformative radical force within participating schools.

This progressive narrative has been critiqued for over emphasising the importance of pedagogical knowledge drawn from oral testimony and singular contexts rather than knowledge developed through a scientific, reason-led approach (Moore & Miller, 1999). Knowledge developed through a scientific research base has been described as "strong knowledge" and pedagogy grown from the views of children and young people labelled "weak knowledge" (Moore & Miller, 1999); the descriptors "strong" and "weak" indicate the interpreted accuracy, utility, and validity of each form of pedagogic knowledge development. A further critique to the empowerment/democratic conceptualisation of pupil voice is that a liberationist approach is adopted, where the views of children are given so much attention and impact that pupils appear to have to make all decisions for themselves, experiencing confusion arising from too much freedom (Freeman, 1996).

High performance/policy technology

The high performance/policy technology narrative for pupil voice can be viewed as an antidote to these critiques, as children and young people are not consulted as a moral obligation. Instead, pupil voice can be actioned alongside knowledge gleaned from a scientific research base, as both types are useful in the pragmatic endeavour to improve the overall functioning of the school. Arnot and Reary (2007) propose that this is better conceptualised as "pupil consultation" (p. 321). Various authors in the field of pupil voice have drawn parallels between "corporate culture" and "school culture" where pupils are consulted in much the same way a manager may consult their staff before making final decisions about change within a company (Vainker, 2021; Levin, 2000; Mosley, 1993). As such, this conceptualisation views pupil voice as a means to an end for providing quality education.

The dominant critique of this narrative is politically driven, situated within a wider critique of the application of neoliberalism to educational policy (Czernaiwski, 2010). High-stakes educational contexts are seen as putting pressure on school staff to ensure good exam performance, and pupil voice, reduced to an aide, is side lined (Fielding, 2001). Pupil engagement activities, such as circle time, are distrusted, as they have been lifted directly from human resources management techniques where the focus is on humans as tools for production (Levin, 2000; Mosley, 1993). As a result, trust between teacher and pupil can break down (Czernaiwski, 2012).

These two narratives reflect conflicting conceptualisations of pupil voice and accompanying rationales for engaging in voice work with children and young people. Educational professionals find themselves teaching in an increasingly competitive school system where innovative means of improving school performance will be valued. Pupil voice is a useful tool for this challenge. Likewise, it is unusual for individuals to engage in the all-consuming work of teaching if they are not concerned with engaging pupils in a deeper way. Pupil voice offers a moralistic avenue for attempting such an endeavour. It is for you to decide which narrative appeals best to you in the development of your own voice practice.

Reflective activity

Now that you are aware of person centred/empowerment and the high performance/ technology narratives conceptualising pupil voice, it is time consider your own views on the matter. Do you think of pupil voice as an action rooted in the values of democracy and equality? Or do you view pupil voice as a great way to improve your teaching and the performance of the school? It may be that your own conceptualisation of pupil voice falls somewhere between these views.

Use the Likert scales in Figure 2.1 to analyse how you conceptualise what pupil voice is. Circle the number for each set of statements that matches your own thoughts.

Pupil's views are always valuable					Pupil's views are valuable if they are useful for improving educational practice				
1	2	3	4	5	6	7	8	9	10
Listening to children and young people is a radical act					Listening to children and young people is a pragmatic act				
1	2	3	4	5	6	7	8	9	10
Listening to children empowers them to become democratic citizens					Listening to pupils empowers educational professionals to improve teaching and learning				
1	2	3	4	5	6	7	8	9	10
I feel a moral obligation to engage in Pupil Voice work					I feel a practical obligation to engage in Pupil Voice work				
1	2	3	4	5	6	7	8	9	10

Figure 2.1 Rating scale.

Types of pupil voice

In understanding what pupil voice is, it is important to understand what *type* of pupil voice you are listening to. Typologies of pupil voice indicate *what* is being listened to, as well as why it is being listened to. They outline salient aspects of pupil voice. Understanding different types of pupil voice can help you identify the form of pupil voice that is important for your practice. Put simply, what is it you are seeking to understand by engaging with the perspective of the children and young people you work with?

Arnot and Reary (2007) outlined four types of pupil voice: classroom talk, subject talk, identity talk, and code talk.

- Classroom talk – This refers to styles of communication and specific forms of language used in a learning environment required to understand what is communicated. This type of pupil voice is likely to be of interest to a teacher if they have concerns about how they communicate and to what extent this conveys their intent to their pupils. They may wish to seek pupils' views about communication styles used by themselves and other adults, versus communication styles pupils use, and then make meaningful changes accordingly.

- Subject talk – This indicates the various rules for how speech and communication should occur in each educational subject. For example, "science talk" refers to the way a pupil should form sentences and the type of vocabulary used when expressing scientific knowledge in a subject, such as physics. A teacher concerned with subject talk as a type of pupil voice in their classroom may be interested in assessing how fluent pupils are at conversing and expressing themselves within the discourse rules of a particular subject.

- Identity talk – This type of discourse is how individuals use different language rules and codes to display their social identities. It involves "casual friendship talk," social bonding, and use of humour. Identity talk is developed outside of the context of school but begins to occur in the school and classroom context. A teacher would be interested in exploring identity talk if they want to understand how pupils view themselves as social characters in relation to others.

- Code talk – This type of verbal exchange refers to how "recognition rules" (Bernstein, 2000) mean that to fully participate in knowledge construction and exchange, pupils need to be able to understand the rules of communication: the pacing of information sharing, how knowledge is selected, and how it is evaluated.

These four types of pupil voice help an educator identify how they communicate with pupils and how pupils communicate with them (classroom talk), the rules of communication (code talk), how pupils are expected to communicate differently in different subject lessons (subject talk), and the personalised language pupils use to express their social identities to others (identity talk). The benefit of this approach is that pupil voice is not viewed as a unidimensional construct. When you say you are interested in pupil voice what are you really interested in? Do you want to explore how pupils demonstrate their understanding of curriculum material (classroom talk/subject talk)? Are you concerned with how pupils view the communication rules of the classroom and whether this acts as a barrier to participation (code talk)? Or, are you interested in pupil's perceptions of self and how these relate to social categories at play in the social world of the school (identity talk)?

Reflective activity

Typologies of pupil voice and associated philosophical and sociological theory that underpin them can appear complex, abstract, and esoteric. This activity therefore focuses on exploring Arnot and Reary's (2007) four types of pupil voice as they would appear in a real-world teaching context. The idea is to create some examples of each type of pupil voice to further demonstrate them. In the four quadrants in Figure 2.2, you will find an example verbal expression of each type of pupil voice. You can reflect on why these have been placed in each category and whether you agree with each categorisation. Add spoken examples of pupil voice from your own real-world observations.

Try not to get too caught up in whether you have categorised a spoken example as the "right" type of voice. Think of this application of the typology of pupil voice as a framework for developing our own understanding. As such, it is to be used to promote and extend your own interpretation of the pupil voices you encounter. It is not about academic "accuracy" or "fact."

Classroom talk	Subject talk
Example: "Yes, sir" (Used to answer and address the teacher)	Example: "I hypothesis that..."
Record your own examples:	Record your own examples:
Identity talk	Code talk
Example: "That lesson was lit."	Example: "I need to complete my homework to a high standard to demonstrate my knowledge"
Record your own examples:	Record your own examples:

Figure 2.2 Examples of different types of classroom discourse.

The role of policy and legislation

Arguably, the rise of pupil voice as a concern for educators has been driven by its representation in policy and legislation in the latter part of the 20th century and beginning of the 21st century. The United Nations Convention on the Rights of the Child (1989) (Article 12) spearheaded this, stating that any child able to form their own views should be able to freely express them and have them given due consideration. This shift towards viewing pupil voice as a right was also reflected in the Children Act (1989), which similarly declared that children, including those with complex needs and communication needs, should have their views established. Children should not be viewed as incapable of partaking in decisions that affect them. This view has remained consistent in subsequent iterations of policy and legislation. For example, the Children and Families Act (2014) places pupil voice as central in processes, such as education and healthcare plans.

However, bold statements in policy and legislation should not be assumed to translate smoothly into real-world educational practices. Situational pressures such as time, expertise, and financial limitations can mean that pupil voice becomes an activity of simply "getting the child's voice" (Burman, 2017, p. 127). This harks back to Arnstein's ladder of citizen participation, and the critical distinction between tokenistic, tick box voice activities, and citizenship rights. Burman (2017) re-creates this argument by critiquing the UN Convention on the Rights of the Child (1989) as allowing adult professionals to claim they are "giving voice" to the child when in effect they are simply re-creating existing power structures by controlling who gets to "speak" and when.

In consideration of such critiques and influenced by the UN Convention on the Rights of the Child, Lundy (2007) created a rights-based model of participation that should have the following elements in place to fully meet children's rights to voice:

Space – There must be a safe and inclusive space for children to share their voice. This does not just refer to physical space but also "space" for children to be heard in a non-tokenistic way.

Voice – Voice does not just mean verbal talk. Children can express their views in a variety of ways, and adults must facilitate this.

Audience – Due consideration needs to be given to who is listening to the child and why.

Influence – How are the children's views that have been collected used? They must have a genuine and meaningful impact to have influence.

The Lundy model has found traction in social care settings and child welfare practices (Kennan, Brady, & Forkan, 2019).

Reflective activity

Lundy's model of participation is a great way to audit existing pupil voice practices and programmes to ensure they are meaningful and not just tokenistic. Choose an example from one of your own methods for collecting and responding to pupil voice or a schoolwide initiative. Use the following audit tool to make an evaluation:

Space

How do pupils know they can give their views? Do they know how and when to give their views?

Do pupils know what will happen to their views? Do they feel they will be acted on?

After answering these questions, rate out of 10 to what extent pupils have a safe space for giving their views (10 being highest and 1 being lowest). __/10

Voice

How do you support pupils to express their views? What methods are used?

What options do pupils have beyond verbal communication to express their views?

How inclusive are your methods? Can any child absolutely express their views without further adaptations being made to the chosen methods?

After answering these questions, rate out of 10 to what extent pupils have a range of inclusive methods available to them to express their views (10 being highest and 1 being lowest). __/10

Audience

Who is responsible for listening to and responding to the pupils' views collected? Why are these people responsible?

Who else needs to be considered as important in accessing pupils' views?

Who doesn't need to involved in the sharing of collected pupils' views? What controls are in place to ensure the right people are involved?

After answering these questions, rate out of 10 to what extent the correct individuals have access to collected pupils' views (10 being highest and 1 being lowest). __/10

Influence

What is done with knowledge gained from pupils' views? How are pupils' views used?

Who takes responsibility for ensuring that pupils' views are integrated into changes in educational practices?

What concrete examples can you give where changes have occurred as a direct result of exploring pupils' views?

How are pupils informed of the impact of their voice?

After answering these questions, rate out of 10 to what extent pupils' views lead to meaningful change (10 being highest and 1 being lowest). __/10

Final score: Add up your score for each of the four considerations (__/40). The higher your score, the more you feel that you have been engaging in pupil voice work in a way that mirrors the lofty aims of policy and legislation, often adapted and applied in misguided ways in applied contexts. If you feel more could be done, then the Action Plan activity at the end of this chapter is a good place to start.

Practice focus: Co-production

Naomi Boswell and Erica Douglas-Osborn

Position statement

Naomi Boswell

Having a voice is something that I have always found to be essential. Before presenting this practice focus, I think it is important share how my experiences have shaped my understanding of voice. My voice allowed me to decide at age 10 what secondary school I would attend, despite this being difficult for my parent. It allowed me to speak up when things were challenging during my high school years. This was not just about having a voice but about knowing it was going to be listened to. It helped me to feel empowered and promote the understanding of my needs.

During my career in education, I have seen some children and young people (CYP) be heard more than others and have become aware that there are many situations whereby CYP are asked their views, but that information is not then acted upon. It has become clear to me that when CYP do not feel listened to or do not see themselves as meaningful participants, their mental well-being and their engagement with society can be affected.

Where there is opportunity for CYP to be involved and heard, I have found that they have contributed innovative ideas and had fantastic new perspectives on how to overcome problems. These "magical" moments ignited a passion and a sense of vitality in me to ensure CYP can participate fully to bring about positive change for them and for others.

What is co-production?

In Chapter 1, Arnstein's model of citizen participation (1969) was outlined with three levels of citizen participation. As authors, we question how effective and meaningful it is to give total power to others and instead propose the notion of co-production. Co-production is not about donating all the power to one party but instead working collaboratively to create a shared understanding and change. Whilst practitioners may feel that they offer opportunities for CYP to have a voice, we propose that sometimes there are little opportunities to move beyond the level of tokenism (Kilkelly et al., 2005). Practice is frequently defined by the actions of adults rather than CYP identifying their own concerns and solutions, with CYP being consulted later in the process and not always then being provided with feedback around decision-making (Tisdall, 2017). Participatory ethical and legal frameworks strive for services created "by service users for service users" – this is also known as co-production (Brandsen, Verschuere, & Steen, 2018)

There is little research exploring co-production with CYP within educational services in comparison to the health and care services (Boswell & Woods, 2021). Perhaps this derives from educational organisations traditionally approaching teaching as a "knowledge transmission" endeavour rather than favouring more inquiry-based learning environments (Johnson, 2010; Chu, Reynolds, Tavares, Notari, & Lee, 2017). It could be suggested, however, that education which facilitates CYP to be knowledgeable and empowered, to build the services they are a part of, and to support them to see their voice as both valuable and valid is essential to broader educational aims and democratic citizenship (UN, 2001).

If we think back to my earlier example of picking what secondary school I went to, I can remember being the only one of my friends who chose where they wanted to go. For most it was their parents and carers who had the final choice. The school I chose took me away from my best friend and also meant that I was going to a school that sought academic success when I was arguably an "average" student. An adult may determine that this decision was not a good one. After all, I was removing a protective factor during a big transition, therefore my parent could have been tempted to make the choice themselves and chose what they thought was best for me without considering my views. Even when CYP are asked their opinion about their lives, how often do they have the final say in the decisions that affect them?

The first step within participation and co-production is about being open to change. Services and practitioners need to be open to doing things differently and be willing not only to listen to CYP but be then willing to act upon the information they are given. Within this chapter and the work we have conducted we choose to define co-production as "an equal relationship between people who use services and the people responsible for services. They work together from design to delivery, sharing strategic decision-making about policies, as well as decisions around the best ways to deliver services" (National Co-production Advisory Group, 2016, p. 1). Participation refers to the involvement of children and young people in decision-making, whereas co-production refers to the co-ownership within these decision-making processes.

Co-production of services: A real-life example

Between summer 2019 and 2020, the authors set out on a co-production journey to work with CYP in one local authority to determine if they wanted an educational psychology service and, if so, what that service should look like. This insightful piece of action research led to substantial changes in thought, practice, and action (Boswell, Douglas-Osborn, Halkyard, & Woods, 2021). CYP determined how they wanted to work with us and how they wanted to share their thoughts and ideas.

The following factors were identified as being important in making the co-production project successful. For each factor there is a reflective activity that will help you think about how you could engage in your own co-production project.

Participation from the beginning

A key part of co-production is involving CYP from the very beginning. Our first step was to determine if CYP even wanted an educational psychology service, and if they did, how would they like to be involved in developing it. In order to do this, we consulted with an established local youth council. This was not the only CYP we went to, but it was a starting point. We explained what the service looked like in other areas and asked whether this is something they would like in their local area. Once they shared that they would like this in their area, we asked if they would like to help us develop it and support us in finding lots of other CYP who might also want to help us.

Gaining the views of CYP

Within our research we met with CYP at a time and place that was convenient for them. This meant that some meetings took place during the evening, at weekends, as well as some during the school day. We shared information in advance about what we were going to talk about. As well as being flexible we had to consider how CYP might want to share their views. When we first started the project, one of the first things we asked the youth council was what is the best way of engaging with them and other CYP. They suggested we run focus groups which were interactive and included activities such as drawing, mind mapping, the use of Post-it notes, and some talking. The youngest children who took part in this research were 7 years old, so we wanted to make the activities as fun and exciting as possible. Therefore, when you are engaging in your own project it is really important that consideration is given to how you might gather information with CYP – asking them first how to do this was what we found to be the best starting point.

Representation

Within our research the youth council felt it was very important that they were not the only CYP consulted. They made it clear we should try to involve as many CYP as possible, as well as make a special effort to engage with more marginalised groups. In order to do this, we contacted all local schools, including schools for those with additional needs. We also contacted some other CYP groups, such as a young parents group and the Children in Care Council. By spreading our net far and wide we were able to engage with CYP of a variety of ages and within different contexts.

When engaging in your own co-production project, it is really important to create opportunities for many different voices to be involved, including from those CYP who may be harder to engage with.

Ongoing relationships

Whilst our research project lasted for a year, the educational psychology service continues to work with CYP, reviewing practice, implementing action, and feeding back on what has happened as a result of their and other CYP contributions. There is a dedicated member of staff who leads this work, who regularly engages with local CYP. They have now developed an online system for CYP to feed back on practice. The educational psychology service meets once a term to go through all the feedback and think about what they can do to develop the service further based on this.

An online presence has also been developed, including a website which explains all the co-production and participation work achieved so far. This is updated termly. All these systems that are currently in place were suggested by CYP.

Reflective activity

Use the audit tool in Figure 2.3 to develop a co-production project in your setting.

Ideas for good co-production practice	Implementation: How could this work in your setting?	Priorities: Set some actionable goals
Participation from the beginning		
Developing staffs understanding: • Holding staff training/development for time to think about what co-production is. • Establishing key members of staff who may be interested in co-production work. • Finding a starting point – need to establish which CYP will want to be involved in this project.		
Gaining the views of CYP		
• Consider what opportunities there are within your setting for co-production with CYP. Ask CYP what they want to discuss/develop/what is important to them. • Inform CYP that they have a choice if they want to take part or not and revisit it this at regular time points. • Ask CYP how they want to be involved and when. • Ask CYP how they want to share their views and consider a range of options that involve verbal and non-verbal communication (drawing, writing, speaking). • Provide information in advance so that CYP can form a view. • Tell CYP why you want them to be involved and what you will do with their information. • Consider what CYP are going to get out from being involved in the project and ask CYP how you can compensate them for their time (payment, new skills, accreditation).		
Representation		
• Consider if a range of CYP have been invited to participate – including those with additional needs and from a variety of backgrounds. • Identify ways in which CYP can be supported to participate, e.g. being supported by someone they trust, meeting in a place they feel safe.		
Ongoing relationships and sustainability		
• Discuss ways to ensure that co-production systems that you create can be sustainable. • Identify ways that CYP can provide feedback on a regular basis. • Identify how adults can regularly look at this information and create action based upon it. • Consider ways in which CYP will receive feedback on the ideas they have shared.		

Figure 2.3 Co-production action plan.

Learning points

Whilst we have explored so far why we should be co-producing with CYP and how we did this, it may be helpful for us to reflect on what went well and facilitated the success of this project but also the barriers we experienced.

Learning point 1 – This work can be challenging! The practitioners within this project shared concerns initially about managing the expectations of CYP, not because they didn't want to be able to implement CYP ideas but because they were concerned that the systems they worked within wouldn't allow them. They were also mindful of how they would gather representative views of a wide range of CYP.

Solutions: When working with CYP it is important to establish the boundaries of what you can and cannot change – although you should remain open to suggestions and doing things differently. It is also important to share with the adults involved that they need to be open to different ways of thinking. When we can do this together, we can make services better.

You may have a school council full of CYP who are wanting to share their ideas, but it will be important to also consider how you might support other CYP who may not be represented in this group to share their views. Sharing views and working with adults in this way may not be something that CYP have done before.

Learning point 2 – Practitioners in our project had concerns about appearing intimidating or negative, particularly if they could not put CYP's ideas into place.

Solutions: It would be helpful to think about how within a school setting, where perhaps CYP are used to being directed by adults, you might be able to create an environment that is encouraging of CYP sharing their thoughts. It might be useful to develop some ground rules or a contract in which CYP and adults contribute so everyone can feel confident in what to expect and everyone can feel safe in being open with their views.

Learning point 3 – Practitioners felt that co-production in our project was facilitated by having an appointed individual who could support this work and be a point of contact between CYP and adults.

Solutions: In schools and educational settings, you might want to think collectively with all members of staff, including senior leadership staff, about what co-production might look like in your setting, what you think the barriers may be, how you could overcome some of these, and if there is an identified individual to support this work.

Case study: Claire's voice

Rachel Helme

This case study is drawn from a PhD project that focused on identity work in the context of the low attainment label in mathematics. The definition of the term *identity* was taken from the work of Bishop (2012) on identities in the mathematics classroom. Bishop defines mathematics identity as

> the ideas, often tacit, one has about who he or she is with respect to the subject of mathematics and its corresponding activities. Note that this definition includes a person's ways of talking, acting, and being and the ways in which others position one with respect to mathematics.

(p. 39)

The definition refers to identity as not necessarily something you are (an acquisition), but something you do (an action). Therefore identity, or identity work, is fluid and dynamic, influenced by a person's life history but also negotiated in various social situations. In the UK education system, students are labelled as high, middle, or low prior attainers, usually in relation to high-stakes assessments such as SATs taken at the age of 11 and GCSEs taken at the age of 16. For students who are labelled as low prior attaining, their mathematical identity work – the way they talk, act, and be in relation to mathematics learning – is often interpreted from the viewpoint of another person, for example a teacher or teaching assistant, and the voice of the student themselves can be silent.

The intention of the project was to learn to listen in new ways to the voice of low prior attaining students to understand their own lived experiences of learning mathematics; to view the students as the experts in telling this story over that of their teacher or myself as researcher.

The context of the project was a post-16 college in the UK, during the academic year of 2020/2021, and focused on one student (for whom I will use the pseudonym Claire) and her teacher. In the summer of 2020, due to the disruption caused by the Covid-19 pandemic, the UK government decided that students would not sit for their formal external GCSE examinations but would be allocated grades by their school based on a range of internal teacher assessments. Claire was allocated a grade 3 in her mathematics GCSE by her secondary school, with the grading system going from grade 1 (lowest) to grade 9 (highest) and was therefore labelled as low prior attaining relative to a GCSE pass of a grade 4 or above. As a result, when Claire moved to study in the post-16 college in September 2020, she had to continue to study mathematics in a resit class in an attempt to improve her GCSE grade. The teacher had been teaching the resit class since September 2020, which meant at the start of the project in December 2020, they had been Claire's teacher for three months.

Case study process

My intention for the study was to prioritise the student's own voice when talking about their mathematical identity, which meant that the methods chosen needed to concentrate on the role of the speaker rather than the listener. At the core of the project was working alongside, rather than on, both the student and the teacher participants, and therefore Claire was not seen just as a data source, but also had a voice in the analysis process. In the project, the cycle of activities was as follows (this series of activities happened three times between December 2020 and June 2021):

- Conduct interviews with Claire.

- Analysis for voice using the Listening Guide.

- Share the "I poem" with Claire for her input.

- Discuss the voice findings with Claire's teacher.

As a listener, your own life history will always have an impact on what you hear, and therefore, as well as focusing on the words of the speaker, I made sure to choose a method of analysis that would be explicit in acknowledging the potential bias of the listener. I used the Listening Guide (Gilligan, Spencer, Weinberg, & Bertsch, 2006), a method for analysing the qualitative interview data, which is described as voice-centred and relational, as a pathway into the lived experience by tuning into the coexisting, multivoices of the speaker. The method uses a set of four sequential listenings, each of which focuses the listener in different ways onto the words of the speaker:

- Listening for the plot.

- I poems.

- Listening for contrapuntal voices.

- Composing an analysis.

Interviewing a student/pupil and collecting voice data

Make questions be about something other than the student directly. Rather than "how are you getting on in maths," you might ask "can you tell me about this particular piece of work or lesson." In my project, I set a task to start the conversation with Claire where I asked her to find an image that represented her experiences of learning mathematics, and then asked her to explain to me how and why the image that she had chosen represented this experience. The subsequent conversations followed on from this starting point, and the task was revisited at the end of the project.

Voice data

Sources of voice data can be a written email, open-ended questions as part of a questionnaire, or transcribed from an interview. I suggest you always voice record any interviews so you can focus on the student. Here I will use a small extract of data to demonstrate the Listening Guide, but in reality, all of the responses were put together as one continuous piece of narrative data.

From the task I set, Claire found an image of a maze and explains her choice as follows:

> I have chosen this image because for me my path was not straight at all there was mistakes and a very long way I had to go to achieve my grades and it wasn't always easy for me as I struggled to understand maths therefore this image is a perfect example of how I felt about my experience of maths however during the college period that I am in I am finally understanding maths and being able to recognize and interpret maths. Maths did annoy me at times and it made me feel like I couldn't understand maths but as I kept trying and trying to understand maths it got a lot clearer to me and I felt like I could finally answer questions and be able to get maths it just would of taken me longer to do so. Finally my opinion of maths is that it is a very difficult subject to get and understand and acknowledge but if you just keep trying and keep persevering you can get through the hurdles of maths and you do very well.
>
> *Claire's email, December 2020*

Step 1: Listening for plot

The first listening has two elements: (1) reading through the interview data to listen for the overall plot, and (2) recording and acknowledging your own initial responses. Firstly, reading through all of the data, your attention will be drawn to the dominant themes and type of stories the speaker tells, about whom and located where, as well as the way they talk using images and metaphors. The purpose is to begin to work with the bigger picture of the data rather than the specific details at this stage, an introduction to the landscape of what is being said, so to speak.

Having listened for the overall plot, the listener should then acknowledge their own responses, not necessarily as a form of suppression as you can never be neutral as a listener, but to be explicit about the subjectivities, values, and norms that are brought into the process. I believe this element is particularly important due to the power imbalances that can occur between a student and a teacher, to reflect on the impact that this disparity may have both on the type of answers you may get when collecting data, and how you might interpret the answers.

Reflective activity

What did you notice when you read the email extract? What stood out for you? What were the themes, metaphors, stories being told? What was your personal response? Why do you think you responded in this way?

_____

_____

_____

_____

_____

Step 2: I poems

In this step, the listener focuses on the words of the speaker and how they use the first-person voice in the narrative by creating and inspecting an "I poem." The listener is tuning into how the speaker talks about themselves by isolating the use of "I" in the data. There are two general rules in the creation process: firstly, underline statements of the data that use the pronoun "I" along with the associated verb or verb phrases and any other words that seem important to retain the meaning of the statement; and, secondly, arrange the statements as a list in the order they appear in the text to form an I poem. Having formed the I poem, the listener reads through the poem inspecting for the rhythms, sounds, and changes in tone of voice or associations that they notice, hence identifying potential coexisting voices. The process is subjective and what one person identifies will be different to what another sees, and it may well be that you decide to include another person in the process as a way of capturing the different possibilities.

Reflective activity

Now we will create the I poem by identifying the use of the first-person voice in the data and arranging them in a list. I have started the process using the first four lines, underlining the use of the pronoun "I" and the associated verb phrase.

I have chosen this image because for me my path was not straight at all there was mistakes and a very long way I had to go to achieve my grades and it wasn't always easy for me as I struggled to understand maths therefore this image is a perfect example of how I felt about my experience of maths however during the college period that I am in I am finally understanding maths and being able to recognize and interpret maths. Maths did annoy me at times and it made me feel like I couldn't understand maths but as I kept trying and trying to understand maths it got a lot clearer to me and I felt like I could finally answer questions and be able to get maths it just would of taken me longer to do so. Finally my opinion of maths is that it is a very difficult subject to get and understand and acknowledge but if you just keep trying and keep persevering you can get through the hurdles of maths and you do very well.

Claire's email, December 2020

You will notice that I have included additional words that I felt were necessary to retain the meaning of the statements, you may make a different decision about which words to keep. I have arranged them in the list in Figure 2.4, keeping the order in which the statement appears in the data. Continue with the process to create the complete I poem.

I have chosen

A long way I had to go

I struggled to understand

How I felt about

_____
_____
_____
_____

Figure 2.4 I Poem.

Now read through the I poem. Do you notice any particular ways of talking? What verbs and phrases are used by the speaker? Are there any repeats or dominant themes? Do any verbs phrases have a similar or related meaning?

Step 3: Listening for contrapuntal voices

It is only in this step that the listener should think about their own purpose for the data collection: Why did they collect the data? And what did they wish to find out? In the similar manner to the melodic lines of music that create a symphony, this stage returns back to the full interview data to think about the characteristics of the different voices identified in the previous step and how they work together in an orchestra of voice. Reading and rereading the data, focusing on one voice at a time, the listener looks for evidence of each voice, adapting and refining where needed. Underlining or highlighting the examples of each voice in a different colour allows the listener to see how the various voices work together in harmony (or not) to highlight how different aspects intertwine to form a person's lived experience.

Reflective activity

The next stage returns to your reasons for collecting the data and what you had hoped to find out. Using what you had noticed in step 2, look at the data and see how the voices are characterised. For example, I noticed in the I poem the use of the verb "to struggle" which I characterised as times when Claire was talking about difficulties in mathematics. I also noticed the verb "to feel" and wondered about her emotional responses. I reread Claire's narrative and underlined the discussions about struggle and double underlined emotional responses.

> I have chosen this image because for me my path was not straight at all there was mistakes and a very long way I had to go to achieve my grades and <u>it wasn't always easy for me as I struggled to understand maths</u> therefore this image is a perfect example of how I felt about my experience of maths however during the college period that I am in I am finally understanding maths and being able to recognize and interpret maths. <u>Maths did annoy me</u> at times and <u>it made me feel like I couldn't understand maths</u> but as I kept trying and trying to understand maths it got a lot clearer to me and I felt like I could finally answer questions and be able to get maths it just would of taken me longer to do so. Finally <u>my opinion of maths is that it is a very difficult subject to get and understand and acknowledge</u> but if you just keep trying and keep persevering you can get through the hurdles of maths and you do very well.

Are there other voices that you noticed in step 2? Can you add to the data by underlining or highlighting these other voices? It might be that some statements or parts of statement fit with more than one of the voices you have identified.

Now look at how all the voices interact. Do any voices work together to tell a story, or do they contradict each other? What is said and what is missing? I noticed that the emotion and the struggle were often part of the same statement, which could suggest that they are intertwined – learning maths is not only about doing but also feeling, a personal response that may need to be supported.

Step 4: Bringing it all together – Composing an analysis

The final step brings all the previous listenings together to synthesise what has been learnt about the speakers. It may well be that you have been able to answer the question that you asked initially or that something else has become apparent, but most likely new questions will have arisen.

Reflective activity

As you revisit the purpose of collecting this data, what have you learnt about the student? What voices did they use and what story has this told you?

Step 5: Sharing findings

In this project, it was important for me to share with Claire the I poem created in step 2 for her input into the analysis process. I did not specifically ask her to identify voices in the poem, but instead asked her the more general question of what she noticed when she read the poems, what had stood out for her. Having their voice listened to is the moral and legal right of every student, but listening without action makes the process tokenistic – listening for listening's sake (see Chapter 1).

The final step of the cyclic process involved sharing Claire's voice with the classroom teacher to enable them to reflect and respond to what was said. These conversations were stimulated by Claire's identity work that the teacher had observed in the classroom, including their own reflections on previous interactions, as well as the work that she had completed in assessments. I brought to the conversation the voice of the student from my analysis and the insight this might give to Claire's identity work in relation to mathematics. The conversations were framed as a discussion between peers, in this case the classroom teacher and a researcher who had previously been a teacher, but this could have been a discussion between colleagues in the same mathematics faculty. The key to the process was having the opportunity to talk about a student and their identity work, and being informed by the student's own voice.

Listening to student voice is important, but so is how you respond. You cannot be sure that your view of what they mean would be the same as the student. Make sure to check with the student themselves to make sure that you have not misinterpreted anything. There are a number of ways you can begin to respond to the student voice activity:

- You might decide to look at a piece of your student's work or think about observations from the classroom. What was revealed by the voice activity? Do you see anything differently as a result?

- You could talk through with a colleague. What can you identify by discussing the activity together?

- You may decide to repeat the activity to see if there are any shifts over time.

Findings

Claire's voice told stories about the struggle of mathematics but also how much she had progressed during her time at the post-16 college. She repeatedly highlighted the move from struggle to understanding and as a result her emotional responses to learning mathematics shifted. She moved from talking about herself in a global view as someone who was not able to do mathematics at all, to someone who was able to be successful in areas of her mathematics learning. She was aware that there would be some topics of mathematics that she could not yet understand, but felt that with hard work and support from her college teacher these difficulties might be overcome. During my conversation with her teacher, they also talked about Claire's successes, reflecting on and challenging their previous assumptions about her identity work in the classroom. In a similar way to Claire, the teacher moved from a global view of a student who would not be successful in mathematics to recognising issues in more specific areas such as difficulties with questions that related to money. The process of reflecting with another, in this case a researcher, and engaging with Claire's own voice allowed the teacher the time and space to reflect on their global assumptions about students labelled low prior attaining in mathematics.

Key takeaways

- The Listening Guide student voice activity would be useful to use with a sample of students that you are particularly interested in or are tracking over time.

- The Listening Guide is a set of guidelines not a strict structure and therefore some parts of the activity may seem a bit ambiguous. You should include each step but can make your own judgements, for example about what additional words to retain for the I poem.

- You should be aware of your own values and judgements that could impact what you notice.

- Sharing back with the student and discussing with colleagues adds colour to the findings.

Chapter summary

Pupil voice work is not as simple as listening to pupils daily and nodding one's head in agreement. Engaging in pupil voice work involves you digging deep to unearth the reasons that led you to working with children and young people in the first place, an orientation towards valuing young minds. Even when pupil voice is used as a useful tool for improving teaching as part of school improvement initiatives, it still cannot escape a humanising effect; it requires acknowledgement that children have experiences and perspectives all their own.

Regardless of your motives, it is likely you will have a natural curiosity towards a certain type of pupil voice, influenced by your own teaching experiences. Ultimately, it is for you to figure out what pupil voice means to you and how you wish to go about engaging with it.

Action plan

Use the tool in Figure 2.5 to develop a plan of how you will engage with pupil voice in your own school/educational context.

PLAN			
ETHOS Why are you developing pupil voice practices?		**GOALS** What do you want to achieve?	
DO			
TASKS Break your goal into discrete tasks to be completed	**TIME LIMITS** Set a realistic time for your tasks to be completed by	**RESOURCES / ACTIONS / ACTIVITIES** What resources will you use? Who is responsible for doing what?	**COMPLETED** Tick this box when each task has been achieved.
REVIEW			
WHAT WENT WELL?	**WHAT WOULD YOU DO DIFFERENTLY?**	**WHAT ARE YOUR ONGOING PLANS FOR DEVELOPING PUPIL VOICE PRACTICES?**	

Figure 2.5 Pupil voice action plan.

Further reading

The International Journal of Student Voice (https://ijsv.psu.edu/) – This is an open-access research journal, which means that it is accessible to all, as content is not hidden behind a paywall. The articles reflect the journal's ethos of voice, as submissions come from all members of the learning community. There are also interesting multimedia projects and practitioner's reflections available.

Student Voice Revolution: The Meaningful Student Involvement Handbook by Adam Fletcher – This is a great book for those seeking further practical ideas and methods for engaging with student voice, as it is written with lots of worked examples of student engagement.

References

Arnot, M., & Reay, D. (2007). A sociology of pedagogic voice: Power, inequality and pupil consultation. *Discourse: Studies in the Cultural Politics of Education, 28*(3), 311–325.

Arnstein, S. R. (1969). A ladder of citizen participation. *Journal of the American Institute of Planners, 35*(4), 216–224.

Bernstein, B. (2000). *Pedagogy, symbolic control, and identity*. Washington, DC: Rowman & Littlefield.

Bishop, J. P. (2012). "She's always been the smart one. I've always been the dumb one": Identities in the mathematics classroom. *Journal for Research in Mathematics Education, 43*(1), 34–74.

Boswell, N., & Woods, K. (2021). Facilitators and barriers of co-production of services with children and young people within education, health and care services. *Educational & Child Psychology, 38*(2), 41–52.

Boswell, N., Douglas-Osborn, E., Halkyard, T., & Woods, K. (2021). Listening to children and young people: An educational psychology service co-production journey. *Educational Psychology in Practice, 37*(4), 1–17.

Brandsen, T., Verschuere, B., & Steen, T. (Eds.). (2018). *Co-production and co-creation: Engaging citizens in public services*. London: Routledge.

Burman, E. (2017). *Deconstructing Developmental Psychology*. Abingdon, Oxon: Routledge.

Children and Families Act. (2014). Available at: https://www.legislation.gov.uk/ukpga/2014/6/contents/enacted [Retrieved: 3 November 2021].

Chu, S. K. W., Reynolds, R. B., Tavares, N. J., Notari, M., & Lee, C. W. Y. (2017). *21st Century skills development through inquiry-based learning*. Singapore: Springer.

Czerniawski, G. (2010). *Emerging teachers and globalisation*. New York: Routledge.

Czerniawski, G. (2012). Repositioning trust: A challenge to inauthentic neoliberal uses of pupil voice. *Management in Education, 26*(3), 130–139.

Fielding, M. (2001). Beyond the rhetoric of student voice: New departures or new constraints in the transformation of 21st century schooling? *Forum for Promoting 3-19 Comprehensive Education, 43*(2), 100–109.

Fielding, M. (2004a). 'New wave' student voice and the renewal of civic society. *London Review of Education, 2*(3), 197–217.

Fielding, M. (2004b). Transformative approaches to student voice: Theoretical underpinnings, recalcitrant realities. *British Educational Research Journal, 30*(2), 295–311.

Fielding, M. (2009). Listening to learners: Partnerships in action conference. In Student Voice, Democracy and the Necessity of Radical Education (Keynote Presentation) 22 April. London: University of East London.

Flutter, J., & Ruddock, J. (2004). *Consulting pupils: What's in it for schools?* London: Routledge.

Freeman, M. (1996). Children's education; a test case for best interests and autonomy. In R. Davie & D. Galloway (Eds.), *Listening to children in education* (pp. 29–48). London: David Fulton.

Gilligan, C., Spencer, R., Weinberg, M. K., & Bertsch, T. (2006). In the listening guide: A voice-centered relational method. In S. N. Hesse-Biber & P. Leavy (Eds.), *Emergent methods in social research* (pp. 253–271). Thousand Oaks: SAGE.

Hart, R. A. (1992). *Children's participation: From tokenism to citizenship.* UNICEF. Available at: https://www.unicef-irc.org/publications/pdf/childrens_participation.pdf [Retrieved: 1 March 2022].

Johnson, A. (2010). *Making connection in elementary and middle school social studies.* London: Sage.

Kennan, D., Brady, B., & Forkan, C. (2019). Space, voice, audience and influence: The Lundy model of participation (2007) in child welfare practice. *Practice*, 31(3), 205–218.

Kilkelly, U., Kilpatrick, R., Lundy, L., Moore, L., Scraton, P., Davey, C., Dwyer, C., & McAlister, M. (2005). *Children's rights in Northern Ireland.* Belfast, Northern Ireland: Northern Ireland Commissioner for Children and Young People.

Levin, B. (2000). Putting students at the centre in education reform. *Journal of Educational Change*, 1(2), 155–172.

Lundy, L. (2007). 'Voice' is not enough: Conceptualising article 12 of the United Nations Convention on the Rights of the Child. *British Educational Research Journal*, 33(6), 927–942.

Moore, R., & Muller, J. (1999). The discourse of ''voice'' and the problem of knowledge and identity in the sociology of education. *British Journal of Sociology of Education*, 20, 189–206.

Mosley, J. (1993). *Turn your school round.* Wisbech: LDA.

National Co-production Advisory Group. (2016). *Co-production: The ladder of participation.* London: Think Local Act Personal (TLAP).

Children Act. (1989). Available at: https://www.legislation.gov.uk/ukpga/1989/41/contents [Retrieved: 3 November 2021].

The United Nations Convention on the Rights of the Child (1989). Available at: https://downloads.unicef.org.uk/wpcontent/uploads/2010/05/UNCRC_united_nations_convention_on_the_rights_of_the_child.pdf_adal_sd=www.unicef.org.uk.1635952553044&_adal_ca=so%3DGoogle%26me%3Dorganic%26ca%3D(not%2520set)%26co%3D(not%2520set)%26ke%3D(not%2520set).1635952553044&_adal_cw=1635952356016.1635952553044&_adal_id=2a74a74c-5f33-46d5-9c39-443236551745.1635952356.2.1635952550.1635952356.c2c3fed4-1307-4e0c-bcb2-86715d6b933a.1635952553044&_ga=2.242483330.1807402206.1635952355-396140209.1635952355 [Retrieved: 3 November 2021].

Tisdall, E. K. M. (2017). Conceptualising children and young people's participation: Examining vulnerability, social accountability and co-production. *The International Journal of Human Rights*, 21(1), 59–75.

United Nations (UN). (2001, April 17). *General comment No. 1, Article 29 (1), The aims of education* (CRC/GC/2001/1). Available at: https://www.refworld.org/docid/4538834d2.Html [Retrieved: 18 October 2020].

Vainker, S. (2021). From employee voice to pupil voice: Taking the 'high road' from the factory to the classroom. *Journal of Educational Administration and History*, 53(1), 21–34.

Chapter 3

PARENT AND CARER VOICE

Listening to, Understanding, and Acting on Parental and Carer Perceptions and Opinions

Angela Hodgkins

Introduction

This chapter will:

- Outline the importance of parents' and carers' voices.

- Identify barriers to, and facilitators of, parent/carer engagement.

- Investigate power relationships and identify ways of empowering parents/carers.

- Analyse ways of building genuine relationships with parents/carers.

A note about terminology: The term *parents/carers* is used throughout this chapter for ease of reading; however, it represents a diverse range of people and family situations. The word *parents* is commonly used to indicate those who have parental responsibility for a child, whether this is formal or informal (Ofsted, 2011), and it includes parents, grandparents, family members, kinship carers, legal guardians, foster carers, social workers, other professionals, and friends.

The importance of parent/carer voice
Parent partnership

Although there is no legal requirement in the UK, every educational establishment, whether mainstream school, special school, nursery, or preschool, is required to demonstrate "parent partnership." The Schools White Paper (DfE, 2010) and the Field Review (2010) both recognised the role that parents have in children's learning and identified the importance of keeping parents informed of children's progress and attainment. Hence, demonstration of parental engagement has become an important aspect of an Ofsted inspection, and it is recognised to be an indicator of good quality (Wilson, 2018). A good practice publication by Ofsted states that

DOI: 10.4324/9781003165842-3

"the more parents are engaged in the education of their children, the more likely their children are to succeed in the education system" (DfE, 2011, p. 16). In the Early Years Foundation Stage too, an overarching principle is "a strong partnership between practitioners and parents and/or carers" (DfE, 2021, p. 6), for the benefit of children. Hattie's (2009) study suggests that if parents are involved in their child's school life, this is equivalent to adding two to three years of educational input to the child's education. It is clear then that, from the point of view of educational settings, parent partnership is advantageous for the child.

A recent parents' survey revealed that 85% of parents wanted a say in their child's education at school level, but only 59% of parents felt that their voices were heard (Parentkind, 2021). It is interesting to note that levels of parent engagement, which had declined in 2019, rose in 2020 during the Covid-19 pandemic and its associated school closures, due to the necessity of home schooling and the increase in virtual communication between home and school.

All school policies and decisions impact on families' lives in some way, so it is only right that families have a chance to influence these and an opportunity to affect these decisions. Curriculum models in some countries, such as the Te Whāriki curriculum in New Zealand, incorporate parent and community relationships as a key strategic focus (Tesar, Pupala, Kascak, & Arndt, 2017), so parents are involved in all aspects of the curriculum. Giving parents the opportunity to influence policy can shape the way the educational establishment serves community needs. However, recent research from the UK suggests that parents' voices are not always authentically heard (Solvason, Cliffe, & Bailey, 2019) and that most settings practise only traditional parent partnership activities, for example helping on school trips, ensuring that homework is done, and attending parents evenings.

Wilinsky and Morley (2021) term this "doing to" rather than "doing with" parents, as the school decides how parents are to be involved rather than parents being able to influence what happens in school. Consequently, parents are seen as a "support act" to the school (Haines-Lyon, 2018) rather than true partners. Parents are often seen as passive supporters (Tveit, 2009), with schools wanting them to be involved but not to "interfere in their professional domain" (MacNaughton & Hughes, 2011, p. 175). This view makes assumptions that parents' priorities are the same as those of school staff, which may not be the case. It is suggested that there is a notion held by teachers of the ideal parent who conforms to school practices and does not challenge (Solvason et al., 2019), but this means that they are also not able to make suggestions of their own or influence practice, based on their own knowledge, interests, and skills.

Levels of involvement

There are many different types of terminology used for involvement of parents, for example parental involvement, parent partnership, parent participation. Parent participation usually indicates participation in school activities (trips, parents' evening); parent involvement, on the other hand, is usually defined as a more active involvement of parents in the everyday life of the school (Oostdam & Hooge, 2013, p. 339). Parent partnership is a true equal partnership between parent and school, each having equal input into decisions made. Epstein et al. (2019) described six types of parental involvement. These can be useful in helping us to determine where our own practice is and how we might increase and improve involvement. The chart in Figure 3.1 is based on Epstein's types but is adapted here for a UK audience. The idea is that the types of involvement start at very minimal (type 1) and increase towards the bottom of the table.

Reflective activity

Epstein et al.'s (2019) typology of parental involvement can be a useful reflection aid or staff discussion tool.

- Complete Figure 3.1, honestly, for your setting. You could do this alone or you could use it as a group activity within your setting. Give examples of each type from your own experience and reflect on the appropriateness of each type of involvement.

- Which types of parental involvement do you see in your setting? Reflect on how well they are currently working to involve parents in your setting.

- Which level of involvement do you think is ideal? How could your setting move to that level? What could you do?

Type of involvement	Example in practice	Reflection
1. parenting schools and parents understand each other's distinct roles		
2. communicating there are effective forms of home-school communication		
3. volunteering parents are recruited to 'help' or to act as an audience		
4. learning at home ideas are provided for parents to be able to help with homework and other curriculum related activities		
5. decision making parents are involved in decision making and are developed as representatives		
6. collaborating with the community community services are integrated into the educational process		

Figure 3.1 Types of parental involvement (adapted from Epstein, 2019).

Barriers to parental voice and engagement

Since the concept of parents' involvement in educational establishments is widely accepted as being positive, most schools will work to ensure that this happens to the best of their ability. However, there will always be barriers to involvement, some on the part of the school, some on the part of parents/carers/families, and some on other more practical factors. Figure 3.2 identifies some of the factors identified in recent research (Hornby & Blackwell, 2018; Mann & Gilmore, 2021). Some of the more familiar factors are discussed further in this chapter (i.e. assumptions/stereotypes, and parents/carers with English as a second language).

Parent / carer factors	School factors
parents / carers' poor experiences of school	teachers' lack of time
low literacy levels	teachers' lack of confidence
a chaotic lifestyle, forgetting information	opening times unsuitable for working parents
lack of understanding of the link between education and future life chances / no interest	teachers' lack of empathy for families living difficult lives
fear of being identified as not coping, being judged	an over emphasis on school formalities
health issues – mental health / phobias / mobility	office staff can be unapproachable
fear of racism / homophobia	only contacting parents when there is a problem
technology issues – lack of access to the Internet / emails / social media	lack of appreciation of the importance of parents / emphasis on the teacher as 'expert'
English as an additional language	teachers' lack of interest in working with parents
lack of confidence, the teachers are the experts, and they know best	children taking messages to and from school and home that may not be accurate
uncertainty about how to approach staff	lack of training on how to work with parents

Figure 3.2 Barriers to engagement.

However, although Figure 3.2 illustrates a significantly long list of barriers, there is evidence to suggest that parent partnership has improved over the last ten years, and this may be due to the increasing role that schools now have in the community and an acceptance that schools have a responsibility to listen to families and get involved in the social care role (Hornby & Blackwell, 2018).

Assumptions

One of the most significant barriers to parent/carer involvement is that of assumptions made about parents' knowledge. Wilson and Gross (2018) point out that to be really involved in their child's school, parents need to be familiar with the curriculum, to understand policies and procedures, to be able to advocate for their child, and to communicate effectively with school staff. This is a long list of criteria which may be unfair to expect of all parents. There is also a belief that parents/carers will have the same objectives as the school and the notion that they will be capable of, and confident in, engaging and providing their voice. There is an assumption that parents will be able to "control, organise and prioritise their own time and activities" (Wilson & Gross, 2018, p. 322). This impacts on their capability and obligation to supervise homework, hear children read every day, and attend parents' evenings. The imbalance in power between parents and school staff is a factor which is well documented and important, and is discussed later in this chapter.

There is a view that parents' voices are silenced through a failure to create time or space for people to communicate. MacNaughton and Hughes (2011) suggest that this can be unconscious or intentional. A teacher might "silence" a parent by using professional knowledge and expertise, sending the message that the teacher is the expert and the parent could learn from them; but this is an unequal relationship, with the parent having nothing significant to "teach" school staff. Silencing could also be due to a lack of confidence on the part of the teacher, particularly in early career teachers. MacNaughton and Hughes suggest that in many cases, the parents' role is to be a passive recipient of knowledge and to show gratitude, their primary duty being to conform (Solvason et al., 2019).

Case study: Andrea's story

Andrea is a learning support assistant, working in a small primary school in the West Midlands. This is their story:

I once worked at a primary school that had a community of settled travellers nearby. When I started work at the school, I hadn't known there was such a thing as "settled travellers." The community was made up of around six mobile homes housing families from a Roma background. When I arrived at the school, the first of the children from the community, Toby, started in reception class. Toby had not been to a preschool or nursery, and it was clear when he arrived that he had no experience of sitting still. On the occasions that we had "carpet time" with the children, he would get up and run around the classroom, or he would lie down and start wrestling one of the other children.

I am ashamed to admit now that we saw Toby as a problem child, a child who would not adhere to the class rules, a child with behaviour issues. He was different from the other children we had in the class, but he quickly learned how to follow the rules expected in class, and although he came to us with no experience of reading or writing, by the time he left reception class, he had settled and was catching up with most of the children. We had seen Toby as a child who "needed to learn to fit in," and this was the case with the family too. We never saw his father, but his mother, younger siblings, aunt, and cousins came to bring him to school and collect him every day.

The school was trying to teach the children about healthy eating and had sent letters out to parents about what sorts of foods were appropriate for a child's lunchbox. However, Toby's packed lunch every day consisted of a chocolate spread sandwich, a cake, a bar of chocolate, and a chocolate milkshake. Letters home were ignored, so a teacher spoke to Toby's mother about it after school one day. Toby's mother laughed and started adding an apple to the chocolate-based lunch box!

Another issue was absence from school. Toby's attendance was below what was expected, as the family regularly took him on trips during school time to horse fairs and other traveller events across the country. The head teacher allowed this to happen and authorised these trips, as he recognised them as being an important aspect of the child's community. The staff team engaged in some research, and it was then that we began to see the Roma peoples as a distinct culture rather than a lifestyle choice.

The community kept several horses, and Toby, at the age of 5, owned his own horse. He was very interested in anything to do with horses and his teachers used this fascination to support his learning in class. In summer, the class was due to go on a visit to a farm by coach. We showed the children photographs of the animals they would see there, which included horses and donkeys. Toby was excited about the trip, but it was clear that his mother was very nervous about it and reluctant to sign the consent form for him to go. We suggested that she could come with us as a helper, and this is what she did; this was a real turning point. A couple of other parents were able to get to know her and the trip was a huge success. After that point, Toby's mother came to school more regularly, often bringing other family members with her. During my time at the school, we had many of the children from that community go through the school. They all started school as very active, fun-loving children and they all did well. The relationship between school staff and the families was crucial in building a supportive experience.

When each of the male children reached the age of 10, they were removed from school and went to live with grandparents in Wales to work on their farm. They always returned to start secondary school but they completely missed Year 6 (and SATs). The head teacher, who had been very understanding about absences, supported the families in their decision to remove their children after Year 5, and was able to convince the Local Education Authority (LEA) that the arrangement the school had with the community meant that children would have the benefit of five–six years of primary school and that this arrangement was preferable to charging the parents with unauthorised absences and risking damaging the relationship we had worked hard to build.

I believe that the staff and children at the school benefitted from this relationship and learned a lot about a different community. I remember some great times, like when the child's family came to ride their ponies and traps through the playground so the children could watch through the windows. I remember the hugely generous thank you presents we received and tried to refuse. I remember trying to do a painting activity with a 3-year-old girl from the community who was wearing the most beautifully extravagant frilly white dress and trying so hard to prevent it from getting covered in paint! Our experiences were enriched by this community.

Case study reflective questions

- Everyone has prejudices and we all make assumptions about others. Reflect on a time you made assumptions about a child or family. What was the impact on the child, family, and you?

- How can we ensure that our assumptions do not result in discriminatory behaviour?

- There are lots of positives in Andrea's story. What can you learn from this about acceptance?

- The head teacher in the story advocates for the family in his dealings with the LEA. What are the consequences of rules and regulations which are at odds with cultural traditions?

English as a second language

Statistics in the UK show that 8% of people speak English as a second or additional language (ONS, 2011). This means that for a significant number of families, communication in English may be difficult. For families coming into the UK from other countries, culture and customs will also be different and may add to difficulty in communicating. A case study of Southeast Asian parents published by Graham and Shabir (2019) highlighted many problems that families experience because of this. The study describes a young mother arriving in England after her arranged marriage, unable to communicate, alone, and frightened. Graham and Shabir explain how parents like this miss out on the informal day-to-day interactions outside the classroom door and that often the only times that efforts are made to ensure that parents understand what is being said is if there is a problem. Often, teaching assistants are used as translators, which can be helpful. However, the case study by Graham and Shabir points out that these messages can sometimes leak out into the community, resulting in a loss of reputation and, subsequently, a breakdown of trust. In the case study, non-English-speaking mothers who are their children's primary carers were often overlooked, with the English-speaking parent, or even older siblings, being involved in discussions with the school. This difficulty is not limited to spoken communication. There is evidence that facial expressions can be very different in diverse cultures, making communication even more difficult (Tsikandilakis et al., 2019).

According to United Nations Refugee Agency (UNHCR, 2022), at the end of 2020 there were 132,349 refugees, 77,245 pending asylum cases, and 4,662 stateless persons in the

UK. Therefore, it is becoming increasingly important for us to find ways of communicating effectively with non-English speaking families.

Power and empowerment

Giving people a voice is the key to empowerment, so it is important to be aware of power imbalances and to build trust to show that the perspectives of others are both valued and valuable (Prowle & Hodgkins, 2020). Often "partnership with parents" comprises informing them of activities or consulting them about potential changes by questionnaire, which may be tokenistic and may not genuinely seek to understand the perspectives of others (Prowle & Hodgkins, 2020). A research study carried out within an early years setting (Bailey & Blasso, 1990, as cited in MacNaughton, 2011) showed that 60% of parents preferred to talk to staff rather than be given a questionnaire, and this rose to 68% in parents from ethnic minorities. One parent in the study said, "I am so tired of checklists and circling the number corresponding to statements that are not mine, and then some other professional making an interpretation or judgement based on that. And I am frustrated at not being told what happened to the information I provided in the survey" (p. 177). Murray (2019) asserts that to actively engage with parents' voices, we need to define what we mean by voice, find suitable ways of listening, find ways to respond so that people feel listened to, and advocate for those views within the broader policy agenda. Closing the feedback loop (Watson, 2003) by informing parents/carers of the outcomes of their responses is essential if they are to feel that their opinions matter.

The view that parents/carers are their "child's first educator" is one attributed to Vygotsky (Smidt, 2010, p. 74), and it is a term used widely today (Solvason et al., 2019). If this is the case, then the expertise of the child's first educator should be respected and welcomed, but this may not always be the case. Brooker (2010) advocates creating a "triangle of care" between parent, practitioner, and child at the beginning of the relationship, with the triangle creating trust and care between each of the three participants. However, in practice, parents often find themselves with responsibility but no status (Lawrence-Lightfoot, 2012) and it is difficult for them to take some control. MacNaughton and Hughes (2011) suggest that this may be because of teachers attempts to protect their professional discretion from parents' interference. Teachers are accustomed to being shown respect and recognition as professionals and, as their role in the classroom demands control and order, removing some control may be uncomfortable for them (Solvason et al., 2019).

Advocacy

In the case study earlier in this chapter (Andrea's story), there are some interesting dynamics between the family, school staff, and the LEA. It was appropriate in this case for the head teacher to advocate on behalf of the parents/carers to prevent the family from potentially withdrawing from the school system completely. The head teacher, in this instance, held the power and was able to act on behalf of the parents. At times, practitioners can find themselves advocating for the families they work with. This is more common within the early years. For example, nursery staff may well advise parents about benefits or financial support for nursery fees.

Some of the barriers to participation faced by parents/carers can be resolved by utilising another person as an advocate. An example of this, outlined earlier in the chapter, is the use of an English-speaking person to interpret spoken or translate written language. Also, parents/carers who experience mental health problems, lack of confidence, or fear arising from their own poor experiences of school may benefit from having someone who is able to speak on their behalf and "be their voice" (Prowle & Hodgkins, 2020, p. 54).

Policy and legislation

Something as important as partnerships with parents should not be inconsistent and dependent on the opinions of individual staff. The UK government stresses that parental engagement strategies should be an integral part of a whole-school approach (DfE, 2011); however, the guidance is very much based on instructing parents about how to support their children's learning, not about listening to them about their opinions, their needs, and their ideas. This is an example of the power imbalance that suggests that, in school, teachers decide what parents should do.

An area of the school curriculum where parents'/carers' views are crucial is that of relationships education. A guidance document (DfE, 2019) provided for schools stresses the need for parental engagement in preparation for this curriculum area. The document presents case studies of good practice, which include questionnaires for parents and an invitation to a parents' workshop or meeting. The definition of parental engagement in the document is "engagement should involve the school providing clear information to all parents, in an accessible way, on their proposed programme and policy; parents being given reasonable time to consider this information; the school providing reasonable opportunities for parents to feed in their views; and the school giving consideration to those views from parents." However, the guide concludes with the statement "schools ultimately make the final decisions and engagement does not amount to a parental veto" (DfE, 2019, p. 2), a statement which could be interpreted by some schools as a reminder that the schools hold the power.

Building genuine relationships

At times, a questionnaire of parents' views can be tokenistic, a "functional approach" intended to extract information from parents (Solvason et al., 2019, p. 196). In contrast, building genuine respectful relationships with parents/carers is the key to creating opportunities for them to voice their views and influence practice. It is important to remember that what teachers and other practitioners see of parents/carers is just a small part of what is going on in their lives. A parent who does not hear their child read every night may have very good reasons for this. There is value in finding ways of developing relationships so that some of the hidden aspects of their lives can be shared (Prowle & Hodgkins, 2020). There may be needs within the family that the school could help with or family circumstances that could explain a child's behaviour. Similarly, parents may have talents or interests that could be useful in enriching children's learning.

Reflective activity

- Think about as many reasons for the following:
  - A parent never comes to parents' evenings.
  - A parent never hears their child read at home.
  - A parent never speaks to the teacher at drop-off/pick-up times.
  - A parent constantly wants to talk to the teacher at drop-off/pick-up times.
  - Several different family members come to pick up a child each day.
- How can you find out more about the families whose children you work with?

Relationship building often must be achieved through snatched moments at drop-off and pick-up, which is very challenging, so any opportunity to talk with parents/carers should be utilised. Communicating with parents/carers when things have gone well is as important as speaking to them when they haven't. Sometimes, it is easy to fall into the trap of only catching parents to talk to them if there is a problem that we need them to help with. However, giving positive feedback is important in building positive relationships. Sending a postcard home with news about a child's achievement or something kind that the child has done is a great way to cement the bond between home and school. The strength-based approach (SCIE, 2022), common in the health sector, is growing in popularity within the education sector (Lopez & Lewis, 2009). The approach focuses on parents'/carers' capabilities and is based on the belief that there are always strengths in the most challenging of situations. Rather than seeing a family with multiple adversities as a "problem family," the strength-based approach looks for positives. A struggling parent who is withdrawing from a drug addiction and whose child always arrives late can be applauded for getting their child to school every day. Identifying the positives helps us to appreciate and encourage others.

Relationships can be accomplished only through a non-judgemental, supportive approach in which assumptions are re-evaluated. The ability to communicate with a wide range of people (children, families, professionals, etc.) relies on the ability to tune into people and to adapt communication styles to others. Empathy is a crucial aspect of communication and "picking up and reflecting back unspoken signals" (Hodgkins, 2019, p. 47) is a useful tool is getting to know individuals. Empathy is one of the "core conditions" first described by Carl Rogers (1957) (Figure 3.3). Empathy helps us to understand how situations seem to another person, looking at a situation through their eyes or trying to walk in their shoes, therefore it is essential for anyone working with people. There are different types of empathy (Hodgkins, 2019, p. 47), advanced empathy being the most powerful. Advanced empathy involves picking up on unspoken signals, being able to assess a person's mental state. Experienced practitioners do this with children all the time; we "just know" when a child has something on their mind or is feeling anxious; we can spot signs that a child's behaviour could get out of control unless we act now. To be able to do this, however, we need to have a well-established relationship with the other person (Hodgkins, 2019, p. 48).

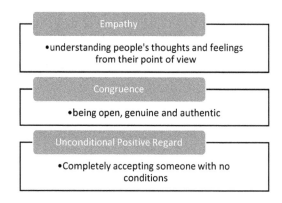

Figure 3.3 Three core conditions (adapted from Rogers, 1957).

Communication is more than just a skill; connecting with others is a fundamental human need (Prowle & Hodgkins, 2020). In an Icelandic study by Einarsdottir and Jónsdóttir (2019, p. 183), a parent of a preschool child explains how much difference it makes to her day if she is welcomed in the morning by the worker who says "good morning, nice to see you" rather than the one who says "(name of child) is here, check." In this study, a good example is described which represents a positive experience of the parent being listened to. In the example, a young boy whose favourite colour is pink has been teased by other children for wearing pink clothes. After the parent's discussion with preschool staff, the preschool organised a "pink day" when all staff and children had to wear pink. The parent's knowledge and views in this instance had been recognised and respected, for the benefit of the child (Einarsdottir & Jonsdottir, 2019, p. 183). This example demonstrates empathy for the child, congruence toward the family, and unconditional positive regard for the child whose preferences are completely accepted.

Case study: Cathy's story

Cathy's background is in primary teaching; she now works at a university as a senior lecturer and researcher, and she is passionate about parent partnership in schools. What follows is her story:

I was in the middle of my divorce and getting the kids out of the house in the morning at about 6 a.m. and getting them back around 6:30–7 p.m. During that hellish time, my ex and I went to a parents' evening where the teacher started with "well his handwriting's scruffy" and then proceeded to annihilate every aspect of my son's (he was about six at the time) character. She had no idea of the turmoil going on in his home life, or how exhausted and broken his parents were.

Case study reflective questions

- Do you think you would have been able to read the signs that these parents were struggling? How would you do that? How important is empathy in this instance?

- How might you become aware of problems like this in a child's home life, whilst working with the child?

- What can you learn about the language you use when talking to parents/carers?

Prejudice and stigmatisation

Hannon and O'Donnell (2021) suggest that there is a tendency for teachers to see parents as different from them, and this, they suggest, is due to class difference in many cases. They propose that there is a deficit ideology amongst teachers in disadvantaged areas, resulting in stereotyping children and families who they believe do not value education and who need to change. The study by Hannon and O'Donnell gives examples of parents being stigmatised because of the area they live in and feeling looked down upon. A parent in the study said, "I felt horrible when teachers tried to understand my child's misbehaviour by probing into my personal life" (Hannah & O'Donnell, 2021, p. 5). This example demonstrates the fine line that professionals need to take to get to know parents without prying unnecessarily; to learn about families' lives without judgement and with sensitivity. Seeing families in need as "problem families" does little to help relationships. Just as we strive to see children as individuals, seeing parents/carers as individual people and listening to their voices is so important. Malm's (2009) research with trainee teachers highlighted the lack of training in personal development, empathy, and collaborative skills. Formal competencies such as subject knowledge and pedagogy are stressed much more, yet building relationships with others is a core aspect of the job. If teachers are to have the confidence to communicate with and listen to parents/carers, then perhaps this should be given more emphasis in their training. Solvason et al.'s (2021) advice is the same for early years practitioners and students, who often find communication with parents very difficult.

Haslip, Allen-Handy, and Donaldson (2019) call for an environment of love, kindness, and forgiveness in care and education relationships between professionals, children, and families. The study is based in the early years and it gives examples of each of the three traits:

- Love – helping a parent to separate from their child by redirecting the child into an activity and reassuring the parent.

- Kindness – thanking parents for their help and giving genuine compliments.

- Forgiveness – forgiving parents for being late to pick up their child.

"Love" may seem an unorthodox choice of word in a discussion about professional working relationships. Page (2018) coined the phrase "professional love" to describe the relationship between early years practitioners and the children and families they work with. She describes it as "professionally loving practice" (p. 130) within a strong, secure attachment which is essential in meeting the emotional needs of a young child.

Reflective activity

- Look at Haslip et al.'s examples of teacher love, kindness, and forgiveness. How do you feel about the ideas presented?

- Can you identify examples of love, kindness, and forgiveness in your own dealings with parents?

Case study: Diane's story

Diane is an experienced practitioner, who works with people with learning difficulties. Here, she talks about her experiences with professionals during the years when her daughter Kerry was exhibiting signs of a developmental disability:

When Kerry started nursery, she wasn't speaking at all, so there were concerns about her starting mainstream education. It was agreed that she would be able to start with a six-week intensive speech and language course that they were just developing at the time. I had concerns at this point because I was seeing a lot of behaviours and tendencies towards autistic behaviour, and Asperger's was at the forefront of my mind. Kerry was becoming more frustrated with not being able to talk and was showing behaviours like lashing out at her siblings.

From nursery into primary, teachers said "it's sibling behaviour," "it's just frustration because she can't talk," "let's try this speech therapy and see how she gets on with that." I didn't really feel my concerns were being listened to. I gave it six–eight months but still wasn't happy, so I asked to speak to the SENCO (special educational needs coordinator) at the school who was also her teacher at the time. All she kept saying was "just continue with the speech therapy," "you need to be doing more at home," and "she's got an older sibling who likes to talk, she's doing all the speaking for her," even though I kept telling them that wasn't the case.

I wanted Kerry to be assessed. When I did eventually get an appointment to see a child psychologist, he said I was reading too much into her behaviour because of my job. He was very judgemental, and I walked out feeling quite deflated because he also said, "We're seeing a lot of people wanting to apply for assessments because they're aware that you can get disability benefits. Is that what you're doing?" That was awful, so I walked out and thought "that's fine, if you're not going to help me, I'll just cope with it myself."

Moving forward about 12 to 18 months, I still wasn't happy at this point. Things had escalated; I was pregnant again and Kerry became quite aggressive because she was frustrated. She doesn't know how to handle frustration and when she was 6 or 7, she wasn't sleeping. She would go 48 hours without sleeping, sometimes 72 hours, and she'd still go to school and manage a full day at school. I don't know how she managed it. The teachers just said, "We'll monitor it, but we're not seeing any of these behaviours in school." And I said, "Well, we all know that girls tend to be able to mask their symptoms,' but when she came out of school, she was running out, running across the road, not seeing any dangers there. And when she was home, then it was affecting her siblings because her sister was being kept up at night and her younger brother was the target for her behaviours; she would be quite aggressive towards him. The GP prescribed a short course of Phenergan to try and get her back into a sleeping routine, which was OK, but that's not the answer, that's not what I was looking for. Kerry was struggling at school, and I was being told that she was 18 months to 2 years behind the others and I said, "So how can we still not be at the point of assessment?" and it really was because she wasn't showing aggressive behaviours inschool.

Luckily a new head teacher came to the school who was passionate about children's mental health and special education needs. Since that point it's been really good; she just spent the time talking to Kerry and seeing what helped her, and the school staff were more accepting. For example, in class when Kerry needed to get up and move around a little bit, they allowed that. They also went away and researched, and found that yellow highlighting really improved children's handwriting and they tried it with her and using yellow textbooks really works for her, so they put all these things into place. We'd have regular meetings, and the new head teacher always had an open door policy, not like before when I didn't feel I could go and approach the head teacher. There's a sense of shame; you question your own parenting. When you go into school and you've got bruises that your child has given you, you don't want to be judged, do you? But the new head teacher was very understanding and accommodating, and I think that made the difference.

Kerry was diagnosed with ADHD when she was 8 or 9, and it wasn't until last year that we had the autism diagnosis, so it has taken quite a while to get that in place because she's 12 now, and I'd been seeing signs since before school age. It's been a real battle. I had to do a ten-week parenting class just to tick the boxes and prove that it wasn't a problem with my parenting. It just leaves you a bit deflated. Now I'm picking up on signs with my youngest child too and I've gone back to the doctor and put that out there on the radar. I know what the systems are now, but it's just finding the energy to go back through it all again.

Case study reflective questions

- What are your immediate thoughts on reading the case study? Is there one part that stands out for you?

- At which points do you think different decisions could have been made?

- How might the story have been different if Kerry's parents had not been so aware of learning difficulties and support systems?

- To what extent do you think teachers should be aware of/involved in problems that are happening at home rather than in school?

- What can you learn from this story about communication and relationships with parents/carers?

Conclusion

This chapter has outlined the importance of listening to the voices of parents/carers, and has considered levels of parental participation, involvement, and partnership. However, whichever level of parent involvement is provided and however much a school or other educational setting wants to get parents/carers involved to hear their voices, there will always be barriers to consider. Some of these barriers are on the part of the establishment, e.g. teachers' lack of time or confidence. Other factors relate to the families themselves, e.g. fear, uncertainty, or language barriers. One of the crucial things to avoid in interactions with parents/carers is making assumptions or stereotyping families. This is an example of Rogers's (1957) unconditional positive regard. The case study by Andrea highlights how stereotyping can be avoided in a school situation, that is by making the effort to get to know families, which is to everyone's advantage. However, this is not always easy if parents/carers have English as a second language, in which case alternative means of hearing the families' voices must be obtained so that they are not disadvantaged.

The issue of power imbalance has been discussed, a challenging concept as schools tend to be based on a hierarchical system and school staff considered to be authority figures. This imbalance means that professionals must seek ways of communicating effectively with families. Often parents/carers are asked for their opinions but this is not followed up with action and change, and parents/carers are not always informed about decisions made based on their feedback. The building of good relationships between staff and families will benefit both parties and the children in our care. It is by taking the time to listen that we learn about families' needs, views, and challenges. This can be a challenge when school staff seldom see parents/carers for more than a couple of minutes at each end of the school day, but tuning into parents/carers by using empathy can help to build trusting relationships. This was especially important for Diane, who describes both poor and good experiences with practitioners in her case study.

As education practitioners, we need to be aware of the power imbalance between staff and parents/carers, and always remember that the parent/carer, as the child's first educator, knows their child best. We all hopefully have the best interests of the child at the heart of what we do, so developing a supportive triangle of care (Brooker, 2010) is the best way to provide child-focused care and education.

Action plan

PLAN			
ETHOS After reading this chapter, do you feel that you create sufficient opportunities to hear and value the voices of parents / carers?		**GOALS** What do you want to achieve?	
DO			
TASKS Break your goal into discrete tasks to be completed	**TIME LIMITS** Set a realistic time for your tasks to be completed by	**RESOURCES / ACTIONS / ACTIVITIES** What resources will you use? Who is responsible for doing what?	**COMPLETED** Tick this box when each task has been achieved.
REVIEW			
WHAT WENT WELL?	**WHAT WOULD YOU DO DIFFERENTLY?**	**WHAT ARE YOUR ONGOING PLANS FOR DEVELOPING PARENT/CARER VOICE PRACTICES?**	

Figure 3.4 Parent voice action plan.

Further reading

- *Making a Difference with Children and Families: Re-Imagining the Role of the Practitioner* by Allison Prowle and Angela Hodgkins – This book is useful for anyone working with children and families. It considers the essential skills and qualities for working with children and families today. Importantly it provides practitioners and students with opportunities to reflect upon what it means to be an effective practitioner through the exploration of theoretical material and practice case studies from a range of professional disciplines.

- Carla Solvason, Johanna Cliffe, and Emma Bailey, 2019, "Breaking the silence: Providing authentic opportunities for parents to be heard," *Power & Education*, *11*(2), 191–203 – This journal article offers an alternative way of looking at parent partnerships in school. It asserts that parents' voices are not heard unless they represent ways that practitioners decide parents should behave. The article calls for a rethink in authentic listening opportunities.

References

Bailey & Blasso in MacNaughton, G., & Hughes, P. (2011). *Parents and professionals in early childhood settings*. London: McGraw-Hill Open University Press.

Brooker, L. (2010). Constructing the triangle of care: Power and professionalism. *British Journal of Educational Studies, 58*(2), 181–196.

Department for Education (DfE). (2010). *The importance of teaching: The schools white paper 2010*. https://www.gov.uk/government/publications/the-importance-of-teaching-the-schools-white-paper-2010

Department for Education (DfE). (2011). *Review of best practice in parental engagement*. https://www.gov.uk/government/publications/review-of-best-practice-in-parental-engagement.

Department for Education (DfE). (2014, updated 2021). *Early years foundation stage (EYFS) statutory framework*. https://www.gov.uk/government/publications/early-years-foundation-stage-framework--2

Department for Education (DfE). (2019). *Statutory guidance: Relationships and sex education (RSE) and health education*. https://www.gov.uk/government/publications/relationships-education-relationships-and-sex-education-rse-and-health-education

Einarsdottir, J., & Jónsdóttir, A. (2019). Parent-preschool partnership: many levels of power. *Early Years, 39*(2), 175–189.

Epstein, J. L., et al. (2019). *School, family, and community partnerships: Your handbook for action* (4th ed.). Thousand Oaks: Corwin Press.

Field, F. (2010). *The foundation years: Preventing poor children becoming poor adults: The report of the independent review on poverty and life chances*. https://webarchive.nationalarchives.gov.uk/ukgwa/20110120090128/http://povertyreview.independent.gov.uk/media/20254/poverty-report.pdf

Graham, A., & Shabir, R. (2019). Lost in translation: A discussion of a small scale study of South Asian non-English speaking parents' experiences of negotiating their children's primary schooling. In J. Wearmouth & A. Goodwyn (Eds.), *Pupil, teacher and family voice in educational institutions: Values, opinions, beliefs and perspectives* (chapter 11, pp. 172–190). London: Routledge.

Haines-Lyon, C. (2018). Democratic parent engagement: Relational and dissensual. *Power and Education, 10*(2), 195–208.

Hannon, L., & O'Donnell, G. (2021). Teachers, parents, and family- school partnerships: emotions, experiences, and advocacy. *Journal of Education for Teaching, 48*(2), 1–5.

Haslip, M., Allen-Handy, A., & Donaldson, L. (2019). How do children and teachers demonstrate love, kindness and forgiveness? Findings from an early childhood strength-spotting intervention. *Early Childhood Education Journal. 47*, 531–547.

Hattie, J. (2009). *Visible learning: A synthesis of over 800 meta-analyses relating to achievement*. London: Routledge.

Hodgkins, A. (2019). Advanced empathy in the early years: A risky strength? *NZ International Research in Early Childhood Education Journal*, *22*(1), 46–58.

Hornby, G., & Blackwell, I. (2018). Barriers to parental involvement in education: an update. *Educational Review*, *70*(1), 109–119.

Lawrence-Lightfoot, S. (2012). Respect: on witness and justice. *American Journal of Orthopsychiatry*, *82*(3), 447–454.

Lopez, S., & Louis, M. (2009). The principles of strengths-based education. *Journal of College and Character*, *10*(4), 1–8.

MacNaughton, G., & Hughes, P. (2011). *Parents and professionals in early childhood settings*. London: McGraw-Hill Open University Press.

Malm, B. (2009). Towards a new professionalism: enhancing personal and professional development in teacher education. *Journal of Education for Teaching*, *35*(1), 77–91.

Mann, G., & Gilmore, N. (2021). Barriers to positive parent-teacher partnerships: the views of parents and teachers in an inclusive education context. *International Journal of Inclusive Education*. Advance online publication.

Murray, J. (2019). Hearing young children's voices. *International Journal of Early Years Education*, *27*(1), 1–5.

Ofsted. (2011). Schools and parents. 3–19. https://www.ofsted.gov.uk/publications/100044

ONS. (2011). ONS census 2011. *Language*. https://www.ons.gov.uk/peoplepopulationandcommunity/culturalidentity/language

Oostdam, R., & Hooge, E. (2013). Making the difference with active parenting; forming educational partnerships between parents and schools. *European Journal of Psychology of Education*, *28*, 337–351.

Page, J. (2018). Characterising the principles of Professional Love in early childhood care and education. *International Journal of Early Years Education*, *26*(2), 125–141.

Parentkind. (2021). Annual parent survey 2021. https://www.parentkind.org.uk/uploads/files/1/Parent%20Voice%20Report%202021%20-%20In%20Full.pdf

Prowle, A., & Hodgkins, A. (2020). *Making a difference with children and families: Re-imagining the role of the practitioner*. Bloomsbury: Red Globe Books.

Rogers, C. R. (1957). The necessary and sufficient conditions of therapeutic personality change. *Journal of Consulting Psychology*, *21*(2), 95.

SCIE. (2022). *Strength-based approaches*. https://www.scie.org.uk/strengths-based-approaches

Smidt, S. (2010). *Introducing Vygotsky: A guide for practitioners and students in early years education*. London: Routledge.

Solvason, C., Cliffe, J., & Bailey, E. (2019). Breaking the silence: Providing authentic opportunities for parents to be heard. *Power & Education*, *11*(2), 191–203.

Solvason, C., Hodgkins, A., & Watson N. (2021). Preparing students for the 'emotion work' of early years practice. *NZ International Research in Early Childhood Education Journal*, *23*(1), 14–23.

Tesar, M., Pupala, B., Kascak, O., & Arndt, S. (2017). Teachers' voice, power and agency: (Un) professionalisation of the early years workforce. *Early Years*, *37*(2), 189–201.

Tsikandilakis, M., Kausel, L., Boncompte, G., Yu, Z., Oxner, M., Lanfranco, R., Bali, P., Urale, P., Peirce, J., López, V., Tong, E. M. W., William, H., Carmel, D., Derrfuss, J., & Chapman, P. (2019). There is no face like home: Ratings for cultural familiarity to own and other facial dialects of emotion with and without conscious awareness in a British sample. *Perception*, *48*(10), 918–947.

Tveit, A. (2009). A parental voice: Parents as equal and dependent – rhetoric about parents, teachers, and their conversations. *Educational Review*, *61*(3), 289–300.

UNHCR United Nations Refugee Agency. (2022). *Asylum in the UK.* https://www.unhcr.org/uk/asylum -in-the-uk.html

Watson, S. (2003). Closing the feedback loop: Ensuring effective action from student feedback. *Tertiary Education and Management*, *9*(2), 145–157.

Wilinski, B., & Morley, A. (2021). Parent leadership and voice: How mid-level administrators appropriate pre-kindergarten parent involvement policy. *Educational Policy*, *35*(7), 1230–1257.

Wilson, D., & Gross, D. (2018). Parents' executive functioning and involvement in their child's education: An integrated literature review. *Journal of School Health*, *88*(4), 322–329.

Wilson, T. (2018). *How to develop partnerships with parents: A practical guide for the early years*. London: Routledge.

Chapter 4

INTERPROFESSIONAL COLLABORATION

The Role of Voice in Working with Other Professionals

Alexandra Sewell

Introduction

This chapter will:

- Introduce interprofessional collaboration as a critical strategy for enabling multiple professionals with differing views and perceptions to meaningfully work together.

- Explore how facilitating teacher professional voice influences feelings of teacher belonging and improved teaching practice.

- Use coaching and self-coaching as a means for you to develop your professional voice and confidence in expressing it.

The role of voice in working with other professionals

The quality social interactions between educational professionals are of increasing importance in creating effective schools. Moolenaar, Sleegers, Karsten, and Daly (2012) attest that "the thesis that 'relationships matter' is currently inspiring educational researchers around the world" (p. pp.355).

When I first began working as an educational psychologist, I visited a wide range of schools and community settings. I quickly realised that the best part of my job was working with people and that the worst part of my job was, also, working with people. Interacting with a range of different professionals was a complex task. Teachers had their own concerns shaped by their unique professional demands. Speech and language therapists had their own language shaped by their unique training. Paediatricians were rarely sighted, shaped by the unique time pressures of their role.

It became apparent to me that the concept of voice work was not just implicit in my collaboration with pupils and parents but with other professionals too. This chapter explores

DOI: 10.4324/9781003165842-4

the complexities of this and will help you develop your own approaches to working with other professionals from both similar and dissimilar training and role traditions.

What is interprofessional collaboration?

Interest in professionals working together in a mutually inclusive and beneficial way has been a subject of interest in healthcare settings and research for the past 50 years (Giess & Serianni, 2018). Multidisciplinary practice is common, defined as more than one person from different professional training backgrounds working in parallel with the same patients (Giess & Serianni, 2018; McIntosh, Dale, Kruzliakova, & Kandiah, 2021). In recent years, researchers and practitioners have been concerned with the further potential of professional collaboration (WHO, 2010). Bronstein (2003) coined the term "interdisciplinary collaboration" in response to this interest and defined it as characteristic of professional's work becoming more enmeshed, leading to the emergence of new professional tasks and problems. It is this concept of interprofessional collaboration that is now of increasing interest in the field of education (Arredondo, Shealy, Neale, & Winfrey, 2004; Borg & Drane, 2019; Bronstein, 2003; Giess & Serianni, 2018; McIntosh et al., 2021; McIntosh, Dale, Kruzliakova, & Kandiah, 2021).

Interprofessional collaboration goes beyond different professionals working in separate silos with the occasional "record sharing" (McIntosh et al., 2021, p. 213). Professionals form an active relationship and begin to learn from and support each other (Arredono et al., 2004; WHO, 2010). There must be shared problem-solving and decision-making, facilitated by a common language, timely information sharing, mutual professional respect, and teamwork (Giess & Serianni, 2018; Stone & Charles, 2018).

Clearly, this is no easy task. There is a critical responsibility for each professional to value the voice of multiple persons from differing educational and skill backgrounds, understanding and responding to perspectives and underlying philosophies that may radically differ to their own (Shoffner & Briggs, 2001). If a tokenistic approach to understanding the voice of other professionals is adopted, then the risk of multidisciplinary, "working-alongside" type practices emerge. If an attempt at meaningful voice work is made, then the lofty aim of interprofessional collaboration has a chance of success.

In an exploration of real-world interprofessional collaboration in education, Stone and Charles (2018) re-emphasised the importance of shared problem-solving, power, and decision-making in ensuring different skills and knowledge are shared across practitioners. They found that school professionals and social workers listed three adults as a minimum and nine adults as the maximum required for successful interprofessional collaboration that would meet a child's needs. They also outlined four forms of collaboration:

- Initiator/coordinator – This professional may not provide direct support to a child, but has the power and oversight to monitor progress and bring different professionals together.

- Assessor – This is the professional who has most input in gathering information about a child and what is currently in place.

- Intervenor – This type of collaboration occurs when a professional implements a specific intervention by working directly with a child or family.

- Whistleblower – This occurs when a professional alerts other professionals in a school about difficulties with personnel directly involved with a child.

These four forms of collaboration can be a useful tool when considering your own educational practice and interactions with other professionals. Are you working in a way that exemplifies interprofessional collaboration? Or perhaps you find yourself repeatedly falling into the role of assessor, or intervenor, or initiator, or whistleblower? The reflective activities in this chapter will help you develop interprofessional collaboration in your practice by focusing on meaningful voice practice.

Reflective activity

Consider Stone and Charles's (2018) four forms of professional collaboration. Contemplate to what extent each role involves listening and responding meaningfully to the views and perceptions of others (see Figure 4.1).

Initiator / coordinator: does this form of collaboration involve listening to the views of other professionals? How could this be achieved in this role?

_____
_____
_____
_____

Assessor: does this form of collaboration involve listening to the views of other professionals? How could this be achieved in this role?

_____
_____
_____
_____

Intervenor: does this form of collaboration involve listening to the views of other professionals? How could this be achieved in this role?

_____
_____
_____
_____

Whistleblower: does this form of collaboration involve listening to the views of other professionals? How could this be achieved in this role?

_____
_____
_____
_____

Figure 4.1 Stone and Charles's (2018) four forms of professional collaboration.

Engaging in interprofessional collaboration

A compelling reason for engaging in interprofessional collaboration and responding to the views and opinions of other practitioners is that school staff must work in an increasingly complex education system with challenging issues. Arguably, a team of professionals is required to solve such problems, as matters arising from real-world complexity are outside of the knowledge and skills of just one professional (McIntosh et al., 2021). Responding successfully to complex situations and pupils' needs also requires time and resources, which are often limited. Engagement in interprofessional collaboration can be a strategic way to make better use of existing resources and increase efficiency (Borg & Drange, 2019).

Considerations for effective interprofessional collaboration centre on this notion of making practice efficient. A critical reflection is whether interprofessional collaboration is always the best way forward and when it isn't appropriate to engage in collaborative efforts (Stone & Charles, 2018). For example, involving professionals without thought about what their role is may result in a situation where roles are not clearly delineated and people don't contribute as a result; a "too many cooks" situation. Who should be involved and what they should be doing/contributing is important.

McIntosh et al. (2021) claim that school nurses are uniquely positioned to initiate interprofessional collaboration. Whilst they may be in a useful position to do so, other professions contest that they are also "uniquely positioned." For example, educational psychologists utilise consultation as a model for practice and are thus heavily dependent on working with other practitioners to complete their work (Arredono et al., 2004). Educational psychologists therefore also claim to be in a privileged position as an initiator and leader of interprofessional collaboration (Arredono et al., 2004; Cameron, 2006). Stone and Charles (2018) interviewed a wide range of professionals who stated that teachers played the most important role in interprofessional collaboration. The authors themselves, however, felt that head teachers we best positioned to initiate and manage collaboration, as they have an overview of the whole school system and the power to instigate change (Stone & Charles, 2018).

These differing perspectives demonstrate that who should be involved and why is an area of important consideration. Further still, contextual factors specific to the school and individual pupils mean that this should occur on a case-by-case basis. The following reflective activity will help you begin to articulate which professionals should be involved in a variety of situations.

Reflective activity

To demonstrate how interprofessional collaboration can be effective Kruzliakova, Dale, Remache, McIntosh, and Kandiah (2021) outlined six educational case scenarios. Read the following two case scenarios and decide which professionals should be involved and why (also see Figure 4.2).

Mathew is a 13-year-old with obsessive-compulsive disorder (OCD). Recently, his symptoms have increasingly affected his ability to complete his schoolwork and stay focused in class. He is also experiencing significant anxiety and absences from school.

(Kruzliakova et al., 2021, p. 273)

Who should be involved? Tick those that apply.

Role		Why should they be involved? What is their role?
Class teacher		
Learning support assistant		
Head teacher		
SENCo		
Educational Psychologist		
School nurse		
Social worker		
School counsellor / MH worker		
Psychiatrist		
Other:		

Figure 4.2 Professional roles and their involvement.

Veronica is a fourth-grade student with below grade level reading ability. She has spent the past 6 years in and out of foster care. In class, Veronica feels self-conscious about reading out loud, and she has a difficult time paying attention. She is also hesitant to make friends and keeps mostly to herself due to fears of being rejected by others. She tends to react aggressively when her classmates attempt to get to know her by asking questions about her family.

(Kruzliakova et al., 2021, p. 274)

Who should be involved? Tick those that apply.

Role		Why should they be involved? What is their role?
Class teacher		
Learning support assistant		
Head teacher		
SENCo		
Educational Psychologist		
School nurse		
Social worker		
School counsellor / MH worker		
Psychiatrist		
Other:		

Figure 4.2 Professional roles and their involvement.

Barriers and facilitators to interprofessional collaboration

When considering your own practice in relation to other professionals it is useful to be aware of and plan for barriers and facilitators to interprofessional collaboration. Planning ahead of time for how barriers can be minimised and facilitators maximised can help ensure success.

A significant barrier is lack of knowledge about different roles held by other professionals (Giess & Serianni, 2018; McIntosh et al., 2021; Shoffner & Briggs, 2001). This can lead to unrealistic expectations about what a particular professional will do (McIntosh et al., 2021). McIntosh et al. (2021) give the example of teachers expecting the school nurse to have detailed knowledge of a child's medical history. Lack of understanding of different professions and unrealistic expectations can also lead to overlap between roles, such as both a school counsellor and educational psychologist being involved in delivering similar-style mental health support (Stone & Charles, 2018).

Communication is another area where barriers to interprofessional collaboration can arise. Information sharing is seen as one of the key benefits of working as a team of professionals, but clarity needs to occur over what information can be shared, by whom, and with whom to allay confidentiality concerns (McIntosh et al., 2021). However, inadequate information sharing can impinge successful group working as not everyone has the correct or complete information they need to achieve agreed outcomes (Giess & Serianni, 2018). When we consider voice practices, a further distinction needs to be made between information sharing and opinion sharing. Beyond the first concern of who you need to share details with, a second is to what extent these are fact-based or personal judgements.

McIntosh et al. (2021) outlined three key facilitators in interprofessional collaboration:

- Senior Leadership Team (SLT) members should reserve time and resources, such as for meetings and workshops.

- School policy should be rewritten or new processes created to integrate a focus on interprofessional collaboration.

- Professionals from a medical background should translate medical and health jargon into layman terms.

Reflective activity

Figure 4.3 is a bullseye diagram detailing barriers and facilitators to interprofessional practice. Consider each barrier and facilitator in turn with regard to your own practice. Colour in to what extent each barrier and facilitator is currently present in your educational voice practice. Colour from the outer circle inwards. Closer to the inner circle should be coloured to represent whether the barrier or facilitator is present. There are also spaces to add your own barrier or facilitator.

Once you have done this, step back from your bullseye diagram. You now have a visual representation of how difficult or easy successful interprofessional collaboration may be in your own practice. Use this reflection to decide your next steps.

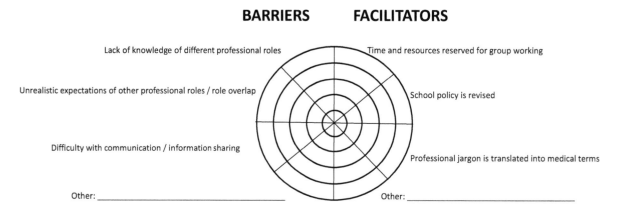

BARRIERS　　　　**FACILITATORS**

Lack of knowledge of different professional roles

Unrealistic expectations of other professional roles / role overlap

Difficulty with communication / information sharing

Other: _____

Time and resources reserved for group working

School policy is revised

Professional jargon is translated into medical terms

Other: _____

Figure 4.3

Focus theory: Teacher voice and teacher-to-teacher relationships

Teachers spend 49.5 hours a week at work (DfE, 2019). If we say an average teacher is getting their recommended 8 hours of sleep a night, that leaves 16 hours per day and 112 hours per week, including the weekend, for living. Of these 112 hours, the average teacher is spending 44.5% of their weekly non-sleeping hours at work. This is almost half of their waking life, holidays excluded. Almost half of their life is spent with their pupils and colleagues.

Some of us get to choose our colleagues, but most of us don't get to decide who we work with. Teachers are spending half their time forging relationships with other adults they do not actively choose to spend such a considerable amount of time with. Arguably, this is a similar experience for other educational professionals.

This is an important consideration when examining teacher voice and its role in teacher-to-teacher relationships. If such a considerable amount of a teacher's time is spent with colleagues, then how they listen and respond to each other's views plays a critical role in the relationships they form and the benefits of positive working collaborations. Yet, teacher voice is a considerably under-researched concept, especially in relation to other voice concepts explored in this book, such as pupil voice, parent voice, and SEND pupil voice. One significant reason for this is that the consideration of teacher voice is yet to appear as a focus concern in educational policy and legislation.

What is teacher voice?

Gyurko (2012) offers one of the few comprehensive conceptualisations of teacher voice, describing it as "the expression by teachers of knowledge or opinions pertaining to their work, shared in school or other public settings, in the discussion of contested issues that have a broad impact on the process and outcomes of education" (p. 4). Teacher voice is expressed in public, and private thoughts and conversations are not considered in this definition. Linking to Chapter 1's discussion of "meaningful voice practice," the perceptions and opinions of teachers also need to be heard and responded to. It is not enough for teachers to merely have thoughts and express them; there needs to be an active listener (Gyurko, 2012). Lastly, Gyurko distinguishes between teacher voice occurring individually or in groups, concluding that group teacher voice is more powerful, such as that organised via a teaching union.

Gyurko (2012) outlined three domains across which teacher voice occurs:

1) Educational voice – opinions and perceptions expressed by teachers relating to pedagogical matters, e.g. assessment, instruction.
2) Employment voice – opinions and perceptions expressed by teachers related to the conditions of their work, e.g. pensions, compensation.
3) Policy voice – opinions and perceptions expressed by teachers related to wider influences that occur outside of the school but influence educational practice within it, e.g. policy and legislation developments, Ofsted frameworks.

These domains for teacher voice can be critiqued as overlapping. For example, Kirk and MacDonald (2001) researched the involvement of teacher voice in two large-scale curriculum development projects in Australia and found that teachers utilised their educational voice as a substitute for lack of a policy voice. Teachers were not agents in the development of new curriculum directions, and so their voices were absent. Yet, when they implemented the new curriculums, they modelled and interpreted them based on their localised knowledge of the contexts they taught in. Kirk and MacDonald concluded that they were "receivers and reproducers of curriculum" rather than "collaborators with other partners in the production of new, school-based instructional discourses" (p. 564). This proposes a subtle but important blending of educational voice and policy voice.

The role of teacher voice in teacher-to-teacher relationships

To create a successful and enjoyable collective teacher culture, teachers need to meaningfully listen to, understand, and respond to the perceptions and ideas of their colleagues (Bjorklund, Daly, Ambrose, & van Es, 2020; Gerlach & Gockel, 2018; Pesonen, Rytivaara, Palmu, & Wallin, 2021; Skaalvik & Skaalvik, 2021). High-quality teacher-to-teacher social interactions influence teachers' abilities to work together to successfully influence educational outcomes, increasing collective belief in what can positively be achieved (Skaalvik & Skaalvik, 2021). They also play a critical role in teacher well-being and retention (Bjorklund et al., 2020). As such, forefronting teacher voice is a useful endeavour as part of wider aims to improve school staff communication systems and relations.

Skaalvik and Skaalvik (2021) found that teacher meetings were the most common forum for teacher voice, as they were used to discuss common school issues and educational problems. Dysfunctional teamwork across meetings led to stress, whereas positive interactions increased job engagement and satisfaction. As such, they argued that "a culture cannot be dictated, but has to result from discussions and common effort" (p. 12), centralising the role of teacher voice. With regard to Early Career Teachers (ECTs), Bjorklund et al. (2020) similarly found that belonging to teacher-to-teacher social networks meant that ECTs felt listened to, valued, and had a sense of belonging that positively influenced their self-efficacy. ECTs tend to report that as they progress through their careers their confidence grows and they see themselves becoming a "little pushy" with regard to making sure their opinions are known to their team members (Skott, 2019, p. 478).

Research has also shown that belonging to particular social groups within a school can affect whether teachers feel listened to and socially included and valued because of this. Gerlach and Gockel (2018) found that belonging to the head teacher's social in-group protected teachers against the negative impact of task conflict, which occurs when staff disagree and are engaged in differing pedagogical practice. Teacher voice was facilitated as those in the head teacher's in-group were more inclined to speak out and share ideas, as the impact of disagreement was mediated through their social relationships with management. In support of this finding, Pesonen et al. (2021) pinpoint the centrality of leader-to-teacher relationships stating that school leaders "play a fundamental role in developing a vision about collaborative working culture, hire staff who are committed to this vision, provide staff development based on shared values, as well as create space for teacher collaboration and sharing responsibilities among staff members" (p. 443).

In summary, teacher voice is integral to positive teacher-to-teacher relationships, which in turn mediate a range of positive educational outcomes (Bjorklund et al., 2020; Gerlach & Gockel, 2018; Pesonen et al., 2021; Skaalvik & Skaalvik, 2021). From their own perspective, teachers report that listening to each other is about developing common and shared goals (Pesonen et al., 2021). This leads to a sense of belonging (Skaalvik & Skaalvik, 2021) and trust that can become so embedded that those engaged in a co-teaching relationship "can tell what the other is thinking" (Pesonen et al., 2021, p. 430).

We all wish to socially belong; it is a fundamental human need. If teachers are to spend so much of their waking time in school forging relationships with colleagues, then the profile of teacher voice needs to be raised. This is especially so for a profession where novel strategies for developing fledgling staff well-being are required (Brady & Wilson, 2021). It is hoped that this chapter has started the journey towards establishing teacher voice on an equal footing with its more prolific voice work counterparts, such as parent voice and pupil voice.

Reflective activity

The aim of the activity is to creatively audit teacher-to-teacher relationship pathways in an educational setting by engaging teacher pedagogical voice. If you are an educational professional who is not a member of a Senior Leadership Team (SLT), consider this activity to be an experiment in raising your voice. If you are an educational professional who is a member of SLT consider, this an investigation into how your staff communicate with each other.

Step 1: Have teachers in your school take some time to think about their practice and to identify one instructional strategy which they think works well. Get them to write this on a card for safekeeping. If you are a teacher engaging in this task independently, do this step for yourself.

Step 2: Ask teachers to share their instructional strategy with a colleague. Do not direct them in how to do this; you want to see how and when they communicate this with others. If you are doing this reflective activity independently, then choose a colleague to share your instructional strategy with.

Step 3: Members of staff who have received information from another teacher about an effective instructional strategy are then to pass this information on to two more teachers. If you are doing this reflective activity independently, wait a week and then reapproach the person you shared with to enquire if it has been shared further afield. This gives you an indication as to how your voice travels within your educational context.

Step 4: Hold a team meeting or use an existing staff meeting. Ask staff to bring their cards upon which they wrote their instructional strategy. During the meeting, staff should share any teaching strategies that they received from others. Write down the instructional strategies and see if you can link them by tracing them back to the originator. Draw this visually and you have a way to see how teacher educational voice spreads between teachers. For additional information about teacher-to-teacher relationships, quiz staff members on how and where they chose to communicate with each other about their practice.

Practice focus: Self-coaching to grow your professional voice

The theoretical and practice focuses of this book have predominantly championed the voice of specific groups and the reflective activities have enabled you to meaningfully promote their voices in education. This practice focus aids you to develop your own professional voice. There is merit in taking time to look inward. The image in Figure 4.4 is of an empty cup. If I told you to drink from it, would you be able to? Of course not. Likewise, if I told you to champion the voices of others without valuing your own, would this be meaningful? Again, of course not.

Figure 4.4

Developing and valuing our professional voice can be daunting. This is especially so for early career practitioners, such as pre-service and Newly Qualified Teachers (NQTs) (Adoniou, 2016; Jones, 2003). The quest to find our voice goes deeper, to knowing and aligning with our personal and professional values. It is part of the complex interpersonal process of expressing and enacting these values. As such, it is useful to have a model of change to adhere to as a guide. Coaching and self-coaching offer applicable models of change.

Coaching and self-coaching

Coaching is a process of reflection that supports an individual to make active changes to a specified area in their life (Adams, 2016; Grant, 2011; Munro, 1999). It often takes place between a coach and a coachee, although group coaching also occurs. The coaching process seeks to challenge the individual by utilising goal setting, focusing on self-motivation and commitment to change, and is time limited (Munro, 1999). Following a coaching model has been shown to increase self-efficacy, a person's belief in their own abilities (de Haan, Grant, Burger, & Eriksson, 2016). As such, it is an apt model of change for increasing someone's value in their own voice and self-efficacy in using their professional voice. By challenging yourself to seek active changes in how you utilise your professional voice, it is highly likely your confidence and ability to do so will grow.

Not every educational practitioner has access to a coach who can guide them through a coaching model process and provide outside perspective and challenge. Paying for a professional coach can be an expensive resource that individuals may not have the means to access. Likewise, the hours coaches generally are available may not meet the availability of a busy educational professional. If you find yourself in this position, then self-coaching is more accessible. Self-coaching involves making a commitment to yourself and the coaching process by using a coaching model to challenge yourself through goal setting and action planning. It is therefore synonymous with giving yourself "space" for self-reflection (Shannon, Snyder, & McLaughlin, 2015; Sue-Chan & Latham, 2004). This is beneficial as it can promote autonomy (Shannon et al., 2015). It is typically viewed as a useful tool for when professional coaching can't occur and is often preferred to peer coaching (Sue-Chan & Latham, 2004).

As self-coaching puts you in conversation with yourself, it is a means of developing your inner voice first before expressing yourself in an external way. It can be viewed as a form of professional voice rehearsal. When we speak out on our own behalf, we typically express ourselves more clearly if we are already acutely aware of our views and perceptions. This empowers us to be direct, which ultimately can mean our professional voice is more likely to be listened to and responded to. There is evidence to suggest that teacher's struggle with assertiveness as a social competency (Milovanović, 2016). Self-coaching offers a self-directed resource for developing teachers' and educational professionals' assertiveness when it comes to sharing their own views and perceptions.

GROW and REGROW coaching models

The coaching process typically follows this structure (Adams, 2016):

- First contact – deciding if coaching or self-coaching is appropriate.

- Contracting – setting boundaries and expectations.

- Second and further sessions – coaching model is followed leading to goal setting, action, and review.

- Review and evaluation – progress is continuously monitored to determine when coaching is no longer necessary.

The GROW coaching model is recommended for its clarity and useability (Grant, 2011). It consists of four interrelated phases:

- Goal – What is it that the individual wants to focus on and change?

- Reality – What is the current situation? Time is spent unpacking current concerns and issues, as well as understanding what may be going well.

- Options – What can the individual do to make change happen? Different options are mind-mapped and explored in depth.

- Wrap up (also known as "way forward" or "wills)": Out of the options generated the most viable are chosen and the individual commits to trying new actions.

The phases do not have to be moved through in a linear way. For example, exploring the reality of a situation can uncover issues that lead a person back to considering goals, and discussing options can lead a person to pick up again on something discussed during reality (Grant, 2011). Grant (2011) also stated that each new session "should start with a process of reviewing and evaluating the learnings and actions competed since the last session" (p. 124). The REGROW model (Figure 4.5) allows shifting between focuses and ongoing reviewing and evaluation:

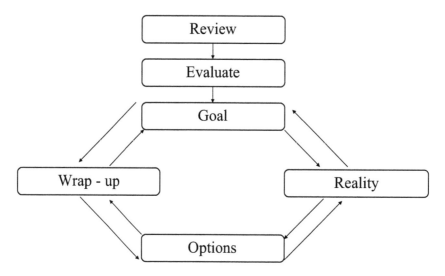

Figure 4.5

The GROW and REGROW models are flexible enough to be used for professional coaching, peer coaching, or self-coaching. This is because they give a simplistic structure which sets direction but does not dictate what individuals wish to explore. The following reflective activity challenges you to engage with coaching to enhance and use your professional voice.

Reflective activity

If you have access to professional coaching, seek to use the process to explore your professional voice. You may wish to recommend the GROW or REGROW model to your coach if you feel drawn to them. If you do not have access to professional coaching, challenge yourself to engage in six weeks of self-coaching and see how your professional voice develops as a result. The following is an adaptation of Adams's (2016) common structure for professional coaching to help you commit to reflecting on your professional voice:

First decision – Firstly, you must decide if self-coaching is appropriate for you and if you can dedicate yourself to getting the most from it. Consider:

- Why do you want to engage with self-coaching?

- What do you wish to develop with regard to your professional voice?

- What are some potential barriers to engaging in self-coaching and how could these be overcome?

Self-support – You need to set boundaries and expectations with yourself. This may sound strange at first, but think back to this chapter's discussion about developing your inner voice before you expand your external, professional voice. If you expect too much of yourself, or from the process, before beginning an inner dialogue you may be at risk of engaging in negative self-talk. Decide when and where you will give yourself the time weekly to complete the coaching process. Name some people you may be able to go to for social support if anything significant arises from the process. Write yourself some positive affirmations centred on encouraging yourself to be brave to engage with the self-coaching process.

Second and further sessions – Ideally, you will set some time aside each week to use the GROW or REGROW model to facilitate your self-reflection. Of course, you will set your own goals. A good place to start, however, is to consider how you currently use your professional voice, what your values are, and what you are seeking to change/achieve.

Review and evaluation – Take time throughout the process to review what changes have occurred with regard to your professional voice and evaluate the impact of these. At a distinct point you may well feel that you have made some substantial changes, e.g. perhaps you are promoting your professional voice more with colleagues. Or perhaps you have found a new way to share your professional voice to engage others. Through this evaluation you can decide when you are ready to end the self-coaching reflective activity.

However, you may find that it is a reflective process you wish to embed permanently into your educational practice.

Case study: Developing my professional voice

In Chapter 1 I gave my position statement and shared that I have personal experience with having my voice heard and acted on, and of not being listened to. I believe this to be a common experience as we move through our careers. Drawing on the ideas of interprofessional collaboration, we rarely get to choose who we work with or have the power to opt out of working with individuals we find challenging (for whatever the reason may be). If we work in a context where there is general respect between staff and employees are meaningfully listened to, then interprofessional collaboration is successful. However, the opposite can also be true. I have found reflecting on my professional voice and use of it to be helpful in mediating these challenges.

When I was a trainee professional, I found it hard to use my professional voice. To some extent this was good, as I clearly didn't know as much or have nearly as much experience as those responsible for training me. Having a quieter professional voice in this context allowed me to demonstrate my reverence for the knowledge of others and made me more open to learning opportunities. However, I also felt that it sometimes put me in a vulnerable position where I was open to critique but could not find a way to respond if my views and values differed. This experience somewhat undermined my confidence as I did not find a way to express my different perspectives, so there was never an opportunity for them to be validated by others or developed through reflective dialogue.

It was through teaching that I gained confidence in the use of my professional voice. As my ability to teach improved through years of practice and skill adaptation, I became surer of my views and perspectives. This surety led me to express myself to colleagues in a more direct way. I used self-coaching to reflect on how I presented myself and concluded that polite but direct was the best method for me to raise my voice, as it was congruent with personality; I find it difficult to be socially performative if it requires me to be duplicitous.

The outcome of this development in my professional voice has been interesting. I find that I speak up more in contexts such as meetings. I have also found that I have gained beneficial outcomes from expressing myself clearly and openly. It appears that sharing my views, even if they are challenging of others, has facilitated change in the workplace that has been beneficial to me. Lastly, even if change doesn't occur through engaging my professional voice, I am not too distressed by this because at least my views are known and cannot be presumed or misinterpreted.

Reflective activity

The purpose of this activity if to consider your own journey with regard to your professional voice. Answer the questions in Figure 4.6 to produce a case study that will help you reflect on your own professional voice.

Think back to a time when you were training as an educational professional. How confident were you in using your professional voice?

_____

_____

_____

_____

How has your use of your professional voice developed as you have come across new experiences in your career? Identify some key experiences and how these influenced your professional voice.

_____

_____

_____

_____

What do you want to further develop with regards to your professional voice and how you use it? How could this be achieved?

_____

_____

_____

_____

Figure 4.6 Professional voice reflection.

Chapter summary

Interprofessional collaboration is increasingly important as a strategy for responding creatively to the complexities of a modern education system. Supporting a child to learn has become more than a case of knowledge transmission, and meeting the needs of pupils requires expertise that cannot be found in one professional alone. Professionals from different training backgrounds will likely have different linguistic, philosophical, and discipline perspectives leading to conflicting views and opinions. Thus, orientation towards meaningful voice practices when working within a multiprofessional team has become a critical endeavour. Further still, when teachers form teacher-to-teacher relationships, valuing teacher voice is also important, as it positively influences a wide range of outcomes. Lastly, whilst it is noble to attempt to understand and respond to the views and perceptions of teachers and non-teaching educational professionals, your own perspectives and how you express them is important too. For interprofessional collaboration and teacher-to-teacher relationships to truly thrive, each individual needs to take responsibility for developing their own professional voice.

Action Plan

Use Figure 4.7 to develop a plan for how you will develop your own professional voice, and an appreciation of and response to the professional voices of your colleagues/staff.

PLAN			
ETHOS Why are you developing your professional voice? / Why do you want staff to develop their professional voice?		**GOALS** What do you want to achieve?	
DO			
TASKS Break your goals into discrete tasks to be completed	**TIME LIMITS** Set a realistic time for your tasks to be completed by	**RESOURCES / ACTIONS / ACTIVITIES** What resources will you use? Who is responsible for doing what?	**COMPLETED** Tick this box when each task has been achieved.

Figure 4.7 Teacher voice action plan.

Further reading

The (Un)official Teacher's Manual: What They Don't Teach You in Training by Omar Akbar – This book covers a range of topics concerning how to get the most out of your teaching career, which broadly relates to developing your values and valuing your opinions. Chapters 4 and 5, "How and When to Say No" and "The Do's and Don'ts of Meetings," respectively, give practical tips on how to use your professional voice in different contexts.

Daring Greatly: How the Courage to Be Vulnerable Transforms the Way We Live, Love, Parent, and Lead by Brené Brown – This book is not specifically about interprofessional collaboration or professional voice but is generally about how we value our own voice to create better relationships with others. The theory and activities are very applicable and valuable to the cause of professional voice.

References

Adams, M. (2016). Coaching psychology: An approach to practice for educational psychologists. *Educational Psychology in Practice*, *32*(3), 231–244.

Adoniou, M. (2016). Don't let me forget the teacher I wanted to become. *Teacher Development*, *20*(3), 348–363.

Arredondo, P., Shealy, C., Neale, M., & Winfrey, L. L. (2004). Consultation and interprofessional collaboration: Modeling for the future. *Journal of Clinical Psychology*, *60*(7), 787–800.

Bjorklund, P. Jr., Daly, A. J., Ambrose, R., & van Es, E. A. (2020). Connections and capacity: An exploration of preservice teachers' sense of belonging, social networks, and self-efficacy in three teacher education programs. *AERA Open*, *6*(1), 1–14.

Borg, E., & Drange, I. (2019). Interprofessional collaboration in school: Effects on teaching and learning. *Improving Schools*, *22*(3), 251–266.

Brady, J., & Wilson, E. (2021). Teacher wellbeing in England: Teacher responses to school-level initiatives. *Cambridge Journal of Education*, *51*(1), 45–63.

Bronstein, L. R. (2003). A model for interdisciplinary collaboration. *Social Work*, *48*, 297–306.

Cameron, R. J. (2006). Educational psychology: The distinctive contribution. *Educational Psychology in Practice*, *22*(4), 289–304.

de Haan, E., Grant, A. M., Burger, Y., & Eriksson, P. O. (2016). A large-scale study of executive and workplace coaching: The relative contributions of relationship, personality match, and self-efficacy. *Consulting Psychology Journal: Practice and Research*, *68*(3), 189–207.

Department for Education. (2019). Teacher workload survey, 2019. *Research Brief*. Available at: https://assets.publishing.service.gov.uk/government/uploads/system/uploads/attachment_data/file/838433/Teacher_workload_survey_2019_brief.pdf [Retrieved: 21 December 2019].

Gerlach, R., & Gockel, C. (2018). We belong together: Belonging to the principal's in-group protects teachers from the negative effects of task conflict on psychological safety. *School Leadership & Management*, *38*(3), 302–322.

Giess, S., & Serianni, R. (2018). Interprofessional practice in schools. *Perspectives of the ASHA Special Interest Groups*, *3*(16), 88–94.

Grant, A. M. (2011). Is it time to REGROW the GROW model? Issues related to teaching coaching session structures. *The Coaching Psychologist*, *7*(2), 118–126.

Gyurko, J. (2012). *Teacher voice* [Unpublished doctoral thesis, Columbia University]. Available at: https://academiccommons.columbia.edu/doi/10.7916/D8FX7HGH/download [Retrieved: 10 December 2021].

Jones, M. (2003). Reconciling personal and professional values and beliefs with the reality of teaching: Findings from an evaluative case study of 10 newly qualified teachers during their year of induction. *Teacher Development*, *7*(3), 385–401.

Kirk, D., & MacDonald, D. (2001). Teacher voice and ownership of curriculum change. *Journal of Curriculum Studies*, *33*(5), 551–567.

Kruzliakova, N. A., Dale, B., Remache, L. J., McIntosh, C. E., & Kandiah, J. (2021). Interprofessional collaboration in school-based settings, part 3: Implementation of IC through case scenarios. *NASN School Nurse, 36*(5), 271–275.

McIntosh, C. E., Dale, B., Kruzliakova, N., & Kandiah, J. (2021). Interprofessional collaboration in school-based settings part 1: Definition and the role of the school nurse. *NASN School Nurse, 36*(3), 170–175.

Milovanović, R. (2016). Assertiveness of prospective teachers and preschool teachers. *Educaţia Plus, 16*(2), 289–303.

Moolenaar, N. M., Sleegers, P. J., Karsten, S., & Daly, A. J. (2012). The social fabric of elementary schools: A network typology of social interaction among teachers. *Educational Studies, 38*(4), 355–371.

Munro, J. (1999). Coaching: An educational psychology perspective. Available at: https://www.researchgate.net/profile/John-Munro-8/publication/237331677_Coaching_An_educational_psychology_perspective/links/5804b1b108ae73d9d6149751/Coaching-An-educational-psychology-perspective.pdf [Retrieved: 19 January 2022].

Pesonen, H. V., Rytivaara, A., Palmu, I., & Wallin, A. (2021). Teachers' stories on sense of belonging in co-teaching relationship. *Scandinavian Journal of Educational Research, 65*(3), 425–436.

Shannon, D., Snyder, P., & McLaughlin, T. (2015). Preschool teachers' insights about web-based self-coaching versus on-site expert coaching. *Professional Development in Education, 41*(2), 290–309.

Shoffner, M. F., & Briggs, M. K. (2001). An interactive approach for developing interprofessional collaboration: Preparing school counselors. *Counselor Education and Supervision, 40*(3), 193–202.

Skaalvik, E. M., & Skaalvik, S. (2021). Collective teacher culture: Exploring an elusive construct and its relations with teacher autonomy, belonging, and job satisfaction. *Social Psychology of Education, 24*, 1389–1406.

Skott, J. (2019). Changing experiences of being, becoming, and belonging: Teachers' professional identity revisited. *ZDM, 51*(3), 469–480.

Stone, S. I., & Charles, J. (2018). Conceptualizing the problems and possibilities of interprofessional collaboration in schools. *Children & Schools, 40*(3), 185–192.

Sue-Chan, C., & Latham, G. P. (2004). The relative effectiveness of external, peer, and self-coaches. *Applied Psychology, 53*(2), 260–278.

WHO. (2010). *Framework for action on interprofessional education and collaborative practice*. Geneva, Switzerland: World Health Organization.

Chapter 5

VOICE PRACTICES TO SUPPORT PUPILS WITH SPECIAL EDUCATIONAL NEEDS AND DISABILITIES (SEND)

Alexandra Sewell, Jane Park, Janchai King, Hannah Fleming, Kara Pirttijarvi, and Stuart Busby

Introduction

This chapter will:

- Inform you of critical developments in meaningful voice work with pupils with Special Educational Needs and Disabilities (SEND) by exploring historical perspectives and current policy and legislation.

- Teach you how to use the grid elaboration method as an adaptive tool for exploring the voice of pupils with SEND (contributed by Jane Park, Janchai King, and Hannah Fleming).

- Present an overview of participatory research and a reflective activity to support you to apply voice tools arising from research to pupils with SEND (contributed by Kara Pirttijarvi).

- Adopt an international perspective on the voices of pupils with SEND by exploring meaningful voice practices in Tanzanian educational contexts (contributed by Stuart Busby).

Critical developments in SEND voice practices

Beyond the momentum of pupil voice is the imperative for voice work that values the perspectives and opinions of pupils with SEND. Pupils with SEND are not a homogeneous group, and how their voices can be supported should not be assumed to be unilateral.

DOI: 10.4324/9781003165842-5

Individuals will require unique understanding and voice practice methods. The SEND voice practices you develop in your educational context should align with the generally assumed idea of inclusive educational practice; some individuals have unique needs that require approaches that are different from and additional to what we provide for a neurotypical child.

Given that you have found your way to this book and this chapter it is likely you already hold inclusion as a professional value. This will orient you towards a considerate application of the voice theories and practices presented in this chapter. Further to this, an understanding of how historically the voices of pupils with SEND have been marginalised, and the developments in policy and legislation that have mitigated this, will further impress the importance of meaningful SEND voice practices.

Historical perspectives

In the 19th and early 20th centuries, educational practices for those we would now categorise as having Special Educational Needs and Disabilities (SEND) were predominantly exclusionary (Sewell & Smith, 2021). Children and young people with identifiable needs, such as visual or physical impairments, were often housed in institutions where some basic education occurred alongside a focus on learning a trade (Morrish, 2013). In this context, even the notion that children and young people have a voice to be valued and respected would have been rare. It was more common for residents of institutions to have their voices monitored and controlled by adults in charge. For example, in one institution for the blind, pupils were restricted to writing one letter a month to a friend or relative (Pritchard, 1963). As such, the concept of voice practices for children with SEND has only established itself in recent years.

Policy and legislation

The following contemporary policy and legislation developments have forwarded the agenda for listening and responding to SEND voices:

- Warnock Report (1978) – The Warnock Report laid out many of the suggestions that led to the development of contemporary conceptions of SEND and support practices. There is no direct discussion of the concept of pupil voice for learners with SEND in the document, however, as the report was such a turning point in the development of inclusion, ideas are present that can be viewed as seeds to the eventual adoption of pupil perspectives as important.

    This is most apparent when Warnock (1978) calls for attitudes towards pupils with SEND to change. The argument was made for the "need for particular attention to the social structure and emotional climate in which education takes place," and that this "may also take different forms" (p. 99). Whilst this is a broad statement, arguably part of the change in social structure and emotional climate that has occurred has been the increasing focus on the importance of SEND pupil perspectives and opinions, and that children may desire different educational arrangements for themselves.

Warnock (1978) pressed that "we cannot overemphasise the urgency of finding ways of changing attitudes so that such people are accepted as ordinary people who merely have certain special needs" (p. 163). Since this was urged, the increasing capacity and interest of educational professionals to understand pupils with SEND by listening to them has been a powerful means for accepting those with educational additional needs as "ordinary" and as being in receipt of their rights.

- The United Nations Convention on the Rights of the Child (1989) (Article 12) – As is also explored in Chapter 2, Article 12 of the UN Convention on the Rights of the Child (1989) stated that all children have the right to hold and express their views "freely in all matters affecting [them]" (p. 5). This had wide ranging influence in the development of pupil voice for those with SEND.

- Children Act (1989) – The Children Act was one of the first pieces of UK-based legislation that actively outlined the role of child voice. Under Section 17, children's wishes had to be regarded before a decision was made as to what services would support them. This had tangible implications for learner's with SEND, as their opinions were to be considered when their educational support was being arranged.

- Children and Families Act (2014) – The Children and Families Act furthered the progression of SEND voices outlining how voice should be included in SEND assessments, such as in education and healthcare plans. The duty was placed on local authorities that they "must ensure that children, their parents and young people are involved in discussions and decisions about their individual support and about local provision" (Special Educational Needs and Disability Code of Practice: 0–25 years, p. 20).

Practice example: The grid elaboration method (GEM)

Jane Park, Janchai King, and Hannah Fleming

Position statement

Dr Hannah Fleming, Dr Janchai King, and Dr Jane Park are Tavistock and Portman NHS Trust-trained educational psychologists working in various schools, settings, and educational psychology services across the UK. Though our working practices differ, we are united by our passionate advocacy for social justice, including enabling and amplifying the voices of children and young people who are more typically marginalised than heard.

What is the grid elaboration method (GEM)?

Messiou (2002) suggests that the process of gathering views of children with SEND is vital to an inclusive education system. However, as highlighted by Smillie and Newton (2020), there is evidence (Lewis et al., 2006) to suggest that there is frequently an element of tokenism when obtaining SEND children's views (as also highlighted in Chapter 2). Mercieca and Mercieca (2014) highlight the pressures of the "runaway world" in which we live and work, advocating for resistance to such pressures; this truly enables listening. The authors also advocate for shifts in practice in relation to the equity of voices, with the aim of ensuring that adults and children are equal partners, enabling the voices and views of even very young children. Taking up this powerful invitation to strive for equity drew the three of us towards novel research and pupil voice methods such as the grid elaboration method (GEM).

The GEM originated in the work of social psychologists Helene Joffe and James Elsey in 2014. Early on, issues of social study using the GEM ranged from climate change to pandemics, earthquakes to urban living. As Joffe and Elsey (2014) describe, the GEM is distinctive in tapping the naturalistic thoughts and feelings that people hold in relation to such issues. They describe how the GEM "provides an instrument that elicits ecologically valid material that minimizes the interference of the investigator's perspective" (p. 173). With its roots in psycho-social research, the GEM has broadened from its original form as a novel research method for eliciting how people think and feel about social and personal issues into a tool for gaining insight into the unique views and experiences of young people. The nature of the GEM, in which material shared by the young person reflects their unique associations to the topic in question, transcends the risk of constraining each individual's narrative inherent in pre-prepared questionnaires (Joffe & Elsey, 2014; Park & Mortell, 2020).

Production of knowledge

Smillie and Newton (2020) highlight potential barriers to young people sharing their views, including supporting learners with communication difficulties or complex needs, the potential power imbalance between children and adults, and encouraging disaffected pupils to give their views. The authors highlight previous research (Norwich et al., 2006) which suggested that one of the most significant challenges when eliciting children and young people's views was the absence of suitable techniques for doing so. This is especially so when working with pupils with SEND.

Thinking dynamically about enabling participation through our social justice lens led us to contemplate moving on from using the GEM as a research tool to applying it in pupil voice work. By using the GEM to elicit young people's views, we hoped to discover more about their thoughts, feelings, and emotional experiences, while contributing to shifting the inherent power imbalance between participant and researcher to a more equitable position.

Using the grid elaboration method

"Doing" a GEM requires no more materials than a piece of paper divided into four sections, which is your GEM grid, and a pen/pencil. It does, however, require an open and curious mind that is fully available to exploring the experiences being described, at a pace that is sensitive and attuned to the emotional states of the child you are working with.

At the top of the GEM grid, provide a visual reminder for the "task," so that the child does not have to remember the instructions and hold them all in mind. In our research, Janchai and Jane adapted the task instructions from Joffe and Elsey (2014) as follows:

> I am interested in what you associate with [experience of transition/Youth Offending Services]. Please express what you associate by using images and/or words. Please put one image/word/phrase in each box. Sometimes a really simple drawing or word can be a good way of portraying your thoughts and feelings.

Topic: My experience of the Youth Offending Service	
Decent key worker	Tiring
	I need money

Figure 5.1 Example of a GEM Grid.

Example grid elaboration method grid

GEM work takes place on a one-to-one basis. It is important to establish with each young person that there are no right or wrong answers, and that there is space for each individual to respond to the GEM grid in whatever ways important and appropriate for them. Therefore, the GEM also requires an investment of time, the creation of a safe space, and well-honed active listening skills.

> There was some variation in the way each young person responded to the GEM grid; some chose to write a few words or a phrase while another drew sketches. Rather than

see this as an obstacle to the collection of useful data, I was encouraged by this, viewing it as a demonstration of how flexible and responsive an information-gathering tool the GEM could be in relation to gaining the views of each unique individual.

(Jane Park)

The next step in the GEM is to support the young person to elaborate on their "associations." Once they had filled in the four boxes, we asked participants to say a little more about each box in sequence, following the order in which they completed each box, so as to trace the order of their associations. This approach ensured that the material to be explored was deeply connected to the unique and personal experience of each participant. Participants were encouraged to take up the freedom to say whatever came to their mind in an attempt to elicit narratives that were structured and defined by implicit and emotive motivations. Rather than applying a set of predefined questions, as in many forms of semi-structured interview, we guided our participants through their initial four associations in order to encourage a fuller exploration of their unique experiences.

The psychoanalytic roots of the GEM are arguably made most explicit when working through the four associations. We drew upon techniques espoused by Hollway and Jefferson (2008, 2012) and Joffe and Elsey (2014) until the point at which each child indicated that they had no more to say about their association. The hope was to empower our research participants and to facilitate exploration of constructs that were personally meaningful to each participant. Some suggested techniques are outlined in Figure 5.2.

Technique	What this looks like
Encouragement	Non-verbal signals such as nodding, active listening skills, consideration of body language and positioning
Parroting	Using the child's own words to encourage further detail; repeating the last words they said to invite further elaboration
Elaboration	Using phrases such as 'tell me more' to encourage the child to elaborate on their associations
Summarising	Showing that you have heard and understood the child's main themes and that you have received them with empathy and unconditional acceptance
Reflecting back/clarifying	Checking your understanding with the child by using phrases such as 'my understanding is…' or 'what I heard was…' and then 'have I understood that correctly/properly?'

Figure 5.2 Listening techniques.

Reflective activity

Finding techniques and phrases that we are comfortable with in relation to pupil voice work is important to its success. Which of the techniques list in Figure 5.2 are already familiar to you? Which feel comfortable, and which would you like to practice and learn more about? How will you practice these skills in a way which feels comfortable and safe to explore?

Extending the grid elaboration method into applied educational practice

The GEM provides educational practitioners a means of eliciting the views of even vulnerable or disillusioned students in a way that would not be available through more direct means. In practice, gaining SEND pupil views has its additional challenges when young people have experienced multiple exclusions from previous settings and are, understandably, defensive (emotionally defended?) against professionals. Professionals can represent authority that they have learnt not to trust; for example, professionals such as social workers may represent an intrusion into their family lives. Similarly, professionals such as educational psychologists have identified them with them SEND, and for many that label was not wanted. Many young people have been multiply excluded from mainstream education, and being asked questions at these times felt like a double-edged sword.

Due to these life experiences, many young people can be sceptical of adults who ask their views via more traditional means. An educational psychology toolkit for gaining views consists of a range of devices, including questionnaires. While questionnaires can provide useful information, they do not provide the richer qualitative information that is so integral to beginning to identify needs and truly understand what is going on in young people's internal worlds.

The nature of the GEM is the space allowed within the framework to think about the qualities of how the child is talking, how they make the assessor feel, and the quality in which they talk about the things most important to them. This makes it highly adaptable for a range of SEND needs.

Reflective activity

Think of a child/young person with SEND that you know well. Think about an area of their life that you would like to know more about. What feelings and emotions are stirred in you when you think about the lived experience of working through a GEM with them?

Case examples

The GEM provides a safe and controlled space for a young person to talk about their views. For these reasons, it is useful in situations of emotionally based school avoidance (EBSA) to gain insight into the reasons why young people have been struggling to attend school. EBSA is rooted in anxiety often related to diagnosed or undiagnosed social communication needs such as autism. Factors including the Covid lockdowns have seen an increase in this and related issues. The role of the educational professional in these cases can be essential to disentangling what is going on in a young person's internal world.

Meet "Ash": A case example from Hannah's educational psychology practice

Ash is a non-binary young person in Year 10. Previously an academic high achiever, Ash came onto my radar due to concerns about a decline in their mental health. Ash had not been attending school for six months, and they began to struggle both with perceived pressures from school and friendships, and their family's reaction to their gender identity. Ash had also recently been diagnosed with autism. Ash and their family had realised the effort Ash had needed to put into masking their difficulties had led to Ash feeling exhausted to the extent they did not want to leave their house. With Ash's consent, I carried out a GEM in the family home, gently asking Ash about their associations to school. Ash chose to fill in each box on the GEM grid with single words: "bad," "noisy," "exhausted," "too much." I was mindful of Ash's physical presentation; they looked tired and sad as they wrote, and when they wrote "too much" I in turn felt like even filling in the grid felt like too much. Sleep was a prominent issue at the time and Ash was clearly very tired. By supporting Ash to elaborate on these four associations, I was able to understand that their recently diagnosed sensory processing needs had contributed to their burn out from school. Being in a noisy, busy classroom had been excruciating for Ash, and Ash's mother reported Ash would come home from school and cry for hours, then sleep. Ash had persevered despite finding this so hard until it became too much. Views and experiences gained through using the GEM informed subsequent advice and intervention for Ash. It was clear that a return to mainstream school was not appropriate or possible at that time.

Meet "Fiona": A case example from Jane's educational psychology practice

Fiona is a 19-year-old young woman who, at the time of my involvement, was out of education. Having previously been enrolled in a specialist college, the upheaval of the pandemic had led her placement to break down. Fiona is autistic and struggled to cope with the changing demands of her learning, physical, and social environments during the pandemic. I drew on the GEM to gain Fiona's views about her wishes for the future. I asked Fiona to describe her first four associations to the question "What is most important to you in your future?" I then asked Fiona to elaborate on each one in turn.

Fiona's four most salient associations, and their elaborations, emerged as follows:

1. To return to college

Fiona let me know that trusting relationships are of fundamental importance to her. "Trust" as a theme recurred throughout our time together, with Fiona describing a need to trust not only the people in her life but to be able to trust in her learning environment. Security and feelings of safety are fundamental building blocks of self-esteem, and this is something Fiona highly valued about her college setting. Fiona described how college felt like a safe place to her, in which she was secure and surrounded, but also free to move around and remove herself from a situation, if needed. Relationships are also key to Fiona. She needs to feel that her needs are fully understood, and that any incidences of emotional dysregulation are understood as strong communications of Fiona's anxiety. She needs to know who she can trust and go to to help her re-regulate and calm, and values staff members who take time to listen and genuinely hear her at the time she needs them. Fiona recognised that the physical and social environment at her college placement enabled her to remain emotionally regulated much more successfully than other learning environments she has experienced in the past.

2. To develop my individual living skills

Back at college, Fiona had begun to work on her individual living skills, including cookery skills and travel training, on a 1:1 basis with a known and trusted staff member. Fiona let me know that she does not like to feel rushed, as this can be anxiety provoking, but equally she is able to articulate her feelings and thoughts, and is able to compromise where needed, so long as this is carefully planned and her voice is heard. Fiona described how she found it difficult to adjust to the staff member teaching independent living skills being in a new role, having previously known him in a different capacity at college. She drew on staff support to manage this transition. In Fiona's words: "I feel strongly that I have so much more to learn and experience with this tutor I already know and I work well with him."

3. To explore craft-based skills

Since attending college, Fiona discovered talents and aptitudes for a range of craft-based activities. She described with enthusiasm and pride how she has created several different pieces of art. Being supported appropriately through the provision of trusting and consistent relationships, a suitable peer group, and a well-managed physical learning environment enabled Fiona to develop her confidence and competence in arts and crafts activities; talents which she had not otherwise uncovered. She felt that she benefitted from a high level of scaffolding and a tightly controlled routine.

4. To keep growing my confidence

Fiona made the very most of her time at college and found the experience beneficial for developing previously unknown art talents and developing her skills in understanding and managing powerful emotions.

Meet "Alfie": A case example from Janchai's work with the youth offending service (YOS)

Alfie is a 15-year-old White British male who was being supported by the local youth offending service (YOS). When I met with Alfie he was very softly spoken and came across as timid. This was a surprise to me considering he was engaging with youth offending services. Perhaps this reflected my assumptions about what kind of young person I would meet during the research. There were times when Alfie's speech was not clear and his use of language meant that I did not always immediately understand what he told me. I found it frustrating at times to try to understand what he was saying and thought that this might be how others feel too. On reflection, I wondered how frustrating it must be to not be able to always make yourself understood by others and whether this may have led to problems with anger that Alfie so openly shared through the GEM. His responses to the GEM when asked about his associations to the YOS were

1. Really good.
2. Helpful.
3. Makes me understand what I did.
4. Helping me think what I'm gonna do before I act.

When supported to elaborate on his four associations, what emerged as really beneficial for Alfie was the way he felt the YOS was supporting him to develop skills in managing anger and thinking before acting. Being able to talk to his YOS worker was expressed as central to this. He related "helpful" to being supported in a practical sense to look for work, while "makes me understand what I did" connected to him working on understanding the potential consequences of his offending. "Helping me think what I'm gonna do before I act" was something he shared he had never done before, associating this positively with his work with his YOS worker. During the process of expanding on his associations, Alfie described the importance of the trusting relationship he began to develop with his YOS worker:

> met [YOS worker] more and more ... I could trust her more and I started, well obviously I started to trust her a lot more every time I met her and spoke to her cos she asked me how things was at home all the time, how's everyone, she was just the only person that understood what was going on really.

Reflective activity

Having read the preceding three case examples, reflect on the production of knowledge. How else might we come to a similar depth of understanding about these young people's lives, perceptions, and experiences? What are the constraints when we use predefined questions or questionnaires?

Summary

The GEM offers a means of exploring SEND pupil views and experiences through visually structuring individual sessions in which the material to be explored is generated by each child/young person's unique and personal associations to the subject of interest. The GEM grid itself functioned as a visual tool, which practice-based evidence shows can be helpful when gaining the views of marginalised voices such as those of autistic young people or of any young people who may otherwise struggle to share their views due to the complex nature of their needs and their experiences. Using the GEM enables rapport to develop, and Hill (2014) and Shepherd (2015) also argue that visually mediated methods may strengthen the communication abilities of young people with autism.

Theory focus: Participatory research

Kara Pirttijarvi

Position statement

I am a 30-year-old White woman who was raised in an Irish-Finnish family in the north of England. I have been bestowed with a wide range of privileges and experiences that have helped me to get to the position I am in today. I previously worked as a primary school teacher and I am now in my final year of study to qualify for a doctorate in child and educational psychology. Across my career in teaching and doctoral study, I have aimed to engage in reflection about my practice and invoke ethical principles to help guide my everyday actions. My actions are also driven by my values, which are steeped in a will to connect with diverse communities and work towards equity for all children and young people.

Knowledge construction

A conscious-raising experience for me has been realising the extent to which the White, Western, adult, male perspective dominates the world of knowledge and knowledge construction (de Sousa Santos, 2007; Fricker, 2007; Hall & Tandon, 2017). Through intellectual colonisation dating back centuries, epistemologies including women's knowledge and African knowledge were silenced in favour of Western, often Eurocentric, paradigms of knowledge (Grosfoguel, 2013). In reality there are countless other ways in which groups, communities, and cultures come to know the world. These include a wide range of world views, traditions, rituals, and languages embedded in indigenous, land-based, spiritual knowledge sharing systems, all of which are equally valid and serve the needs of the communities in which they were established.

Children, including those with SEND, can also be seen as a group whose cultural knowledge has been relegated to the peripheries of knowledge construction. Through tools such as the curriculum, children can get the impression that no other alternative ways of knowing about the world exist. However, there are ways in which educational professionals can acknowledge the existence of inadequacies in the system and show children that there are many perspectives and ways in which the world can be represented. One way is to give children agency over their stories and how they tell them. Not only can this be an empowering force for the knower but may bring meaning to someone else.

Children in research

Over the last 30 years, there has been a shift in how children and childhood have been situated within social science research (Qvortrup, 1993; James & Prout, 2015). Rather than being studied from a distance, children are increasingly being positioned as active participants within investigative processes (Corsaro & Molinari, 2000). In studies spanning areas such as academic learning and health, children have brought perspectives and insights that adults had not anticipated (Barrett, Everett, & Smigiel, 2012; Brady et al., 2015; Mengwasser & Walton, 2013).

There are, however, particular narratives around children that seem to linger. One noteworthy conceptualisation is from the field of law where children are often positioned as "fragile dependants" (Appell, 2009). To echo what is stated throughout this book, to be positioned as somebody with agency in their own life can be a liberating force and have lifelong implications. There are two ways in which education professionals can act to uplift the voices of children with SEND as part of the debate around knowledge democracy:

1) We can question why we focus on adult-centric perspectives and ways in which children with SEND are positioned.
2) We can support children and young people with SEND to develop the sense of agency they feel in their own lives.

Participatory research approaches

Participatory research approaches apply to all children. This section has been placed in the current chapter as participatory research approaches are a particularly useful and applicable tool for pupils with SEND, and they are adaptive and highly considerate of the strengths and needs of the children taking part. As will be revealed through the forthcoming reflective activities, it is critical in participatory research approaches to consider the ways in which the participating children communicate. This means that participatory research approaches are flexible enough to work in a truly collaborative way with pupils with a wide range of communicative and cognitive abilities.

Children's participation in research exists on a continuum (Hart, 1992); their level of involvement can look very different, from being invited to contribute as participants to conducting research themselves (Holland et al., 2010). Both of these examples can be considered participatory because children are involved even though the depth of their involvement differs significantly. Participatory research is therefore considered an approach to research rather than a particular methodology or design (Wallace & Giles, 2019). The origins of participatory research approaches can be traced to research conducted by indigenous communities in the Global South (Hall & Tandon, 2017) and to discourse around knowledge construction rooted in the radical ideas of Paulo Freire (1968).

Supporting children to become researchers themselves is a particularly powerful way to position children as co-creators of knowledge and increase their participation in research. With children at the helm of decision-making, power has been consciously identified and redistributed to children. Children may become empowered through the process, and disseminating their work can lead to transformative change beyond its initial scope (Bagnoli & Clark, 2010).

A great starting place for learning more about how to use participatory approaches is Aldridge (2016), alongside the comprehensive guide to supporting children to become researchers written by Kellett (2005). The work undertaken by the Open University Children's Research Centre, where children and young people are supported to conduct their own projects about topics that matter to them, is also helpful.

Reflective activity

Participatory research approaches aim to address the powerlessness felt by those who experience things being done "to" them rather than "with" them. This can especially be the case for pupils with SEND who can be viewed as lacking in agency because of their disability and/or additional needs. They can be positioned as needing educational provision and intervention to be done to them because of a perspective that they are vulnerable and need protecting, but this can hamper a pupil's personal autonomy. For children who often experience educational events being done to them, it can be liberating for their input to be sought. This starts with asking them whether participation in decisions about their education is even something they want to take part in.

You, as the educator and questioner, have more power within this situation; there is always the possibility that the responder feels they have no choice but to acquiesce. This can be mitigated, to a degree, by asking *if it is OK to ask* before asking formally. When contemplating beginning a participatory research project with pupils, or pupils with SEND, consider who you want to be involved and actively seek to ask them if it is OK to ask them to take part. Use the table in Figure 5.3 to plan who you will ask, record their answer, and reflect on your feelings in response to how they answered. You may feel a bit taken aback if a respondent says no, but remember that a child with SEND feeling able to say no is an act of self-advocacy.

Pupil name	How I asked them to participate	Their answer	How did I feel and respond on receiving this answer	How will I change how I approach and ask the next child to participate?

Figure 5.3 Gaining informed consent.

A Covid-19 participatory research project

Many of us have looked back over the events that unravelled after March 2020 and thought "What happened?" Research into the psychological and emotional impact of the Covid-19 pandemic on children and young people is in its infancy (e.g. Chawla et al., 2021). Reports from organisations, institutions, and charities focused on keeping young people "connected, engaged and mobilised" during the pandemic and emphasised the importance of "[ensuring] that the voices of young people and those that support them do not get forgotten during the crisis" (UK Youth, 2020). Social justice and equity considerations were strong themes amongst these materials, with findings that disadvantaged young people, such as those with SEND, were disproportionately impacted by events of the pandemic (Office for National Statistics, 2020).

Living through these times, it was important to me to focus my doctoral thesis on children and their lived experiences of the Covid-19 pandemic. After exploring the literature base, three things stuck out to me:

1) Reports largely focused on explaining and addressing the impact of the pandemic on young people.
2) Those consulted on their views were largely age 10-plus (generally secondary age).
3) All research had been conducted by adults, meaning adults played a significant role in interpreting children's views.

With requirements to undertake a thesis, I felt I could devote the time and resources needed to conduct research which could fill these gaps. Shifting the focus away from understanding the impact of the pandemic, I wanted to focus on how children had made sense of what had happened. I proposed to my university that I would recruit children as researchers and support them to conduct research with other children to build new knowledge about how children have come to understand the Covid-19 pandemic. Children are more than capable of engaging in the processes of meaning-making about their experiences, and this could be well facilitated by the use of participatory approaches.

Thesis research

Co-research team

I worked alongside five Year 6 pupils (the "co-research team"). Each co-researcher worked alongside a "pupil participant" who was in Year 2 at the beginning of the project and Year 3 at the end. Each co-researcher worked closely with their pupil participant in a research partnership. Together, we conducted a study that used participatory approaches in order to build a theoretical framework rooted in children's constructions of the Covid-19 pandemic.

Co-researchers undertook a lengthy period of preparatory work to build their confidence as researchers: this included a virtual parent/carer Q&A forum, a research skills workshop, and a pilot study. It was very important to the co-researchers that they could build rapport with their pupil participant to enable them to feel confident sharing the pupil participant's pandemic experiences and communicate their thoughts in the most meaningful way.

Reflective activity

Consider your educational setting. What existing resources do you have that would enable you to develop an effective co-research team? Who would be involved as co-researchers and pupil participants and why? How would you structure relationships between co-researchers and pupil participants? Use the space in Figure 5.4 to begin to outline your ideas.

Potential co-researchers	Potential pupil participants
Ways in which co-researchers and pupil participants could meet and work together	

Figure 5.4 Potential co-researchers and pupil participants.

Research process

Consistent with participatory approaches, while I provided some parameters for their research actions, decision-making at each stage belonged to the co-research team. First, they generated their research questions and chose the means by which they could work with their younger partner. In their pilot study, they practised using a range of tools to jointly construct meaning about their experiences of the pandemic (e.g. drawings, painting, Lego, role play, music, journalistic interviewing). Research partners met several times to ensure clarity of understanding and generated a rich and nuanced data set. The co-researchers then undertook a dense period of interrogating, analysing, and abstracting their data to produce a theoretical framework rooted entirely in children's indigenous knowledge.

One of the most important steps of designing the research was the co-researchers' decisions about what tools and materials might best support their participant to express themselves. The co-researchers were keen to choose tools that built upon their partner's preference, seeing this as the best way to build their confidence and perhaps open avenues of thought that would have been otherwise inaccessible. Most of the pupil participants wanted to draw, and the co-researcher drew alongside them. Their collaborative creation of different visual artefacts, drawn while talking, seemed to stimulate dialogue better than any other tool available. Drawing stimulated talking within the safe space of their research partnership, and talking together led to research partners co-constructing their understanding.

Co-researchers undertook data analysis simultaneous to their rounds of data collection. Using a technique known as constant comparative analysis, co-researchers meticulously coded, compared, categorised, and conceptualised their data (Charmaz, 2014). This was a lengthy and iterative process that took place over several days. Through increasingly sophisticated coding procedures, they worked extremely hard to raise their data to higher and higher levels of abstraction, leading them to develop concepts that were integrated into their own theoretical framework.

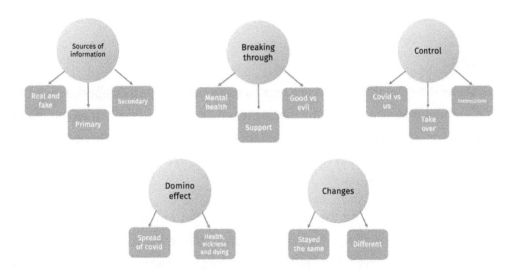

Figure 5.5

Adult influence

The participatory approaches adopted did not only entail the acts of supporting children to become researchers, but involved taking decisive steps to limit my own influence as an adult.

These steps included:

- *Adopting a position of "not knowing."* I knew that I would bring to the research my own biases and assumptions about what children may think, and I adamantly did not want this to impact upon the process. While it is never possible to be completely neutral and get rid of all adult influence, I hoped that I could work towards inhabiting a position of "not knowing" by addressing the biases that I brought with me.

- *Making it clear to the children that my role was one of facilitator.* I worked hard to ensure any decision that could be feasibly taken by the children was indeed taken by the children.

- *Supporting children to stay close to their data set.* The co-researchers undertook the bulk of data analysis so it was important to remind them to stay close to the indigenous perspectives provided by their pupil participant. It is said that the stories that we are told, or tell ourselves, become our reality (Cerroni, 2015) and providing transcripts of all sessions helped the co-researchers to keep rooted in their data.

- *Facilitating equitable participation.* Even within groups of children, inequalities abound. When facilitating voice practices, we need to be aware of the individual differences within the group and our propensity to hear some voices over others. I kept aware of the dynamics within and across groups, intervening where necessary in order to invite reflection from all voices, while also respecting silence as a contribution in its own right.

Challenges

By no means was it a straightforward process to embed participatory approaches (Waller & Bitou, 2011). Dilemmas are constantly encountered and I can reflect on an abundance of ways in which participation could have been increased, especially if there were no constraints on time or information required for ethical approval from university. It can often feel unsatisfactory and frustrating.

And indeed, to err is human and there were errors to reflect on. One that sticks out is when co-researchers were analysing their transcripts line by line. We began our group data analysis session and one co-researcher was keen to share something immediately: she had found something she felt was relevant to the research question and read aloud a quote from her participant. He had said, "I feel like I just changed my mind right now." When asked to elaborate, the co-researcher found it difficult to explain why she felt it to be relevant. It turns out that, when I was transcribing, I had bolded and underlined this quote because I found it interesting myself and had forgotten to reformat it back to normal before printing it out.

Upon reflection, to me this showed the power imbalance enduring within the adult–child relationship. Even when extensively laying the groundwork to communicate that this knowledge and its meaning belonged to them, children perhaps feel a sense of comfort from adults having the "right" answer. It may also speak to broader ideas about supremacy that we look to those perceived to have the most power as the most trustworthy representatives for an objective "truth."

Reflective activity

If you chose to engage in a participatory research project in your educational setting, how could you mitigate against the aforementioned challenges? What other potential obstacles do you foresee and how may they be overcome?

Enacting change

Co-researchers and their participants were conscientious and showed they were committed to every step of the research process. The result is one in which they have co-created and communicated knowledge that represents their understanding of the Covid-19 pandemic and belongs entirely to them. The use of participatory approaches can lead to transformative change, and the co-research team members hope that by disseminating their framework, they can invite others in to understand their reality as children living through a 21st-century global pandemic. They have plans to share this across their school and further afield, hoping their framework may resonate with others, and that some may feel galvanised to conduct their own research too.

Conclusion

Educational professionals are political actors. We play important roles in the process of knowledge construction, and we wield this influence inside the realms of politics and ideology. The ways in which knowledge is produced has political implications, perhaps in maintaining certain power structures or in challenging the status quo. As key players in the world of knowledge sharing, teachers are in exciting positions to be agents of change. Active change is not necessarily about *doing more* but may be more about stepping back a little. By creating that space and resisting the imposition of our own knowledge or belief systems, we can create spaces with more evenly distributed power structures where all contributions can be valued. From personal experience, these spaces are ones in which children can make a real difference, and this especially includes having an impact on the adults around them.

Case study: The use of SEND pupil voice to promote inclusive teaching in the Global South

Stuart Busby

This case study provides an international perspective by exploring the development of innovative voice practices at several educational settings within the Tanga region of Tanzania. These settings are starting to use pupil voice to overcome the many challenges faced in the region by developing a curriculum which is increasingly determined by the views of children with additional needs.

The challenge of inclusion

The Republic of Tanzania in East Africa is the second most populous country in the southern hemisphere. Its population has doubled during the last three decades, and several authors, including Moorosi and Bush (2020), have argued that historically the

Tanzanian government has struggled to develop the quality of leadership needed within its schools to formulate and deliver an effective education policy which caters for the needs of all learners. By failing to deliver effective improvement for the provision of children with additional needs, Harber (2017) suggests that the Tanzanian government has followed the trend of its counterparts in other sub-Saharan countries who also failed to develop effective inclusive education.

Criticism of the Tanzanian government's approach to inclusive education, largely from large multinational companies which began investing in the country during the latter 20th century, led to the publication of policies to focus school leaders on the outcomes that were expected for children with additional needs. The 1995 Tanzanian Education and Training Policy stated, "Every child has a right to proper primary education as a human right regardless of sex, colour, ethnicity and abilities" (Possi & Milinga, 2017, p. 63). Likewise, the Dakar Forum of 2000 called for schools to improve their inclusivity by appointing "well-trained teachers who use active learning techniques; adequate facilities and resources; a local language curriculum; and a welcoming, gender-sensitive environment" (Harber, 2017, p. 54).

However, the clarification of outcomes for inclusion has not led to improved provision. Of the 7.9% of Tanzania's school-aged population who live with a disability, it is estimated by the World Bank (2018) that less than 1% are enrolled in pre-primary, primary or secondary education. Harber (2019) argues that even those learners with additional needs who attend school are excluded because they cannot access the curriculum and teaching in the same way as other learners. Consequently, there is both a high dropout rate and a lower rate of achievement among children with special educational needs. Yahl (2015) suggests the ongoing failure of inclusion in schools has exacerbated problems in society, particularly in urban areas, which have attracted a migration of unskilled adults from rural areas seeking employment.

Armstrong (2002) maintains that the failure of the Tanzanian government's policies on inclusion can be attributed to the lack of resources for staff training to develop strategies to support children with additional needs. He suggests that this does not provide staff with the confidence to gather pupil voice to ensure that learning opportunities are effectively matched to children's interests and needs.

Pearls in the ocean

Despite the limits of government policy, a small number of settings in Tanzania have successfully addressed provision for special educational needs by introducing increasingly innovative approaches. For example, the deputy education minister of Tanzania was glowing in his praise of the Gabriella Children Rehabilitation Centre (Devlin, 2016) for its regular use of an occupational therapy room and provision of prevocational skills programs to support young adults with additional needs. Likewise, Magaoni Primary School in Tanga, which is the only primary school in the region to provide "alternative provision," has received praise for its effective support of children and adolescents with special needs (especially cerebral palsy, Down syndrome, autism, dyslexia, and microcephaly) (Busby, 2021).

Magaoni's head teacher passionately believes that her school's curriculum should be determined by the

> views, feelings and learnings of our children so that they take ownership and pride in their learning. We get to know our pupils well so we can understand how they best learn, how they can best communicate and how best to facilitate opportunities to share their news, views, and feelings.
>
> *(Busby, 2021, p. 24)*

To achieve these aims, regular opportunities are provided to capture the pupil voice of pupils with SEND, including:

- Access to "feelings boards" in each classroom, where children place symbols by their names to indicate their emotions. These are often used by staff to stimulate whole-class discussions about feelings as part of circle times, and work on social and emotional aspects of learning.

- The use of a "family group" system where children with additional needs meet each term to discuss a range of themes and issues, often health and well-being related. Decisions and comments are then passed onto the school board and head teacher. These family groups can also encourage older pupils to care for younger pupils and to become role models.

Figure 5.6

As a result of these strategies and the regular modelling of language, pupils with additional needs feel increasingly confident to share how they feel at incidental times during the day. This leads to improved attendance and achievement.

Widening the net

However, effective use of pupil voice to support the development of inclusive education appears to be the exception rather than the norm in Tanzania. Why is this?

Arguably settings, such as Magaoni, are led by what Tams (2018) would describe as "Heroic headteachers." These individuals have powerful visions and can inspire their followers. In addition, they can operate in a transactional style. At the Gabriella Children Rehabilitation Centre there is an expectation that all staff elicit older student's views and work collaboratively with them to open businesses, such as small restaurants and kiosks, which will employ them once they leave school. By providing their staff with a share of profits from the businesses, the leadership of this setting is successfully reinforcing the conformity needed to successfully implement their shared vision for valuing the voices of children with additional needs.

However, the current hierarchical structure of Tanzanian leadership training does not provide most head teachers with the confidence or skills to develop as heroic leaders. Moorosi and Bush (2020) are critical of leadership programmes, suggesting that their trainers' unwillingness to deviate from the prescriptive content supplied by the City Education Office prevents participants from developing strategies to develop transformational approaches to using pupil voice to make their curriculums more inclusive. This view is supported by Harber (2019) who bemoans the lack of freedom to innovate in Tanzanian leadership programmes.

Arguably the Tanzanian government's more recent imposition of policies to make its schools more inclusive, which some authors such as Thompson (2017) have hailed as a triumph, may have conversely reduced the capacity of school leadership to focus on developing the energy and skills of their staff to make effective use of pupil voice. Yahl (2015) suggests that the primary thrust of these recent policies has been to focus schools on the administration rather than the leadership of special needs provision. This is supported by a Harber's (2019) study of the Inclusive Education Policy, which requires identifying the number of students in each of the country's schools and the number of textbooks they are provided with. As suggested by Dimmock (1999), this expectation from the City Education Office that all head teachers focus on "lower order" administrative duties will reduce the capacity to lead and focus on tasks designed to improve staff, student, and school performance.

The preceding arguments suggest that the extent to which leaders in Tanzania can effectively use pupil voice within their own schools to make them more inclusive is limited. This situation is compounded by factors in wider society which they cannot control. As well as limiting the spread of teacher training, Yahl (2015) suggests that the country's poor transportation network, and the subsequent rural isolation of many families, sustains a culture which actively discriminates against children with additional needs. In many villages it is still common to dehumanise children with disabilities by referring to them as objects. In some extreme cases in rural areas, Harber (2019) has demonstrated how individuals with learning difficulties are "cured" with witchcraft, which sees them tortured, killed, and parts of their bodies taken as good luck charms.

Thus, whilst there are positive examples of the impact of pupil voice to develop inclusive practice in Tanzanian schools, one must bear in mind that the effectiveness of the strategy to develop further has been limited by the significant barriers that exist in all areas of Tanzanian life. One hopes that by sharing examples of the positive impact of pupil voice in settings such as Magaoni, researchers such as myself can further encourage school leaders to adapt similar practice to support their most vulnerable learners.

Chapter summary

Pupils with SEND have unique rights to pupil voice. This is reflective of their unique needs. The examples explored in this chapter have purposefully been chosen for being open and applicable to a wide range of needs, as voice practices should not treat pupils with SEND as a homogeneous group. Voice practices need to be adaptable and sensitive to access individual perspectives. The GEM offers an example of a sensitive tool, as it provides an open framework for pupil voice. Children with SEND can access the process in any way that is meaningful to them. When working with pupils with SEND we also need to consider what true engagement looks like. Participatory research approaches offer an avenue for considering how to involve pupils in a way that potentially avoids being paternalistic. This is an especially radical perspective to take when we consider pupils with SEND who have traditionally not been viewed as having a voice to engage due to their needs, such as children who are non-verbal and use alternative forms of communication. Their views and perceptions still matter, and they need to be offered opportunities not just to have their opinion heard to but set the topic for discussion.

Action plan

Use the following tool to develop a plan of how you will understand and respond to the voices of SEND pupils.

PLAN			
ETHOS **Why are you developing SEND pupil voice?**		**GOALS** **What do you want to achieve?**	
DO			
TASKS Break your goals into discrete tasks to be completed	**TIME LIMITS** Set a realistic time for your tasks to be completed by	**RESOURCES / ACTIONS / ACTIVITIES** What resources will you use? Who is responsible for doing what?	**COMPLETED** Tick this box when each task has been achieved.
REVIEW			
WHAT WENT WELL?	**WHAT WOULD YOU DO DIFFERENTLY?**	**WHAT ARE YOUR ONGOING PLANS FOR DEVELOPING SEND PUPIL VOICE PRACTICES?**	

Figure 5.7 Voices of SEND pupils action plan.

Further reading

The Art of Autism: Shifting Perceptions by Debra Hosseini – This book is a great example of how art and poetry can be used by individuals with SEND to share their voices. It features 77 autistic individuals and their art and poetry.

Eleni Dimitrellou and Dawn Male, 2020, "Understanding what makes a positive school experience for pupils with SEND: Can their voices inform inclusive practice?" *Journal of Research in Special Educational Needs*, *20*(2), 87–96 – This research journal article provides a complete example of how the voices of pupils with SEND can be listened to so that inclusive educational practice is enhanced.

References

Aldridge, J. (2016). *Participatory research: Working with vulnerable groups in research and practice*. Bristol: Policy Press.

Appell, A. R. (2009). The pre-political child of child-centered jurisprudence. *Houston Law Review*, *46*, 703–734.

Armstrong, F. (2002). The historical development of special education: Humanitarian rationality or 'wild profusion of entangled events? *History of Education*, *31*(5), 437–456.

Bagnoli, A., & Clark, A. (2010). Focus groups with young people: A participatory approach to research planning. *Journal of Youth Studies*, *13*(1), 101–119.

Barrett, M. S., Everett, M. C., & Smigiel, H. M. (2012). Meaning, value and engagement in the arts: Findings from a participatory investigation of young Australian children's perceptions of the arts. *International Journal of Early Childhood*, *44*(2), 185–201.

Brady, G., Lowe, P., & Olin Lauritzen, S. (2015). Connecting a sociology of childhood perspective with the study of child health, illness and wellbeing: Introduction. *Sociology of Health & Illness*, *37*(2), 173–183.

Busby, S. (2021). *The impact of professional development on improving the quality of leadership and education within Tanzanian Primary Schools in the Tanga region* (Masters of Arts dissertation, University of Exeter).

Charmaz, K. (2014). *Constructing grounded theory*. London: Sage.

Chawla, N., Tom, A., Sen, M. S., & Sagar, R. (2021). Psychological impact of COVID-19 on children and adolescents: A systematic review. *Indian Journal of Psychological Medicine*, *43*(4), 294–299.

Children and Families Act. (2014). Available at: https://www.legislation.gov.uk/ukpga/2014/6/contents/enacted [Retrieved: 3 November 2021].

Corsaro, W. A., & Molinari, L. (2000). Priming events and Italian children's transition from preschool to elementary school: Representations and action. *Social Psychology Quarterly*, *63*(1), 16–33.

Devlin, H. (2016). Moshi deals with autism in children. *The Guardian*. Available at: https://www.ippmedia.com/en/features/moshi-deals-autism-children-head [Retrieved: 6 March 2022].

Freire, P. (1968). *Pedagogy of the oppressed*. New York: Seabury Press.

Fricker, M. (2007). *Epistemic injustice: Power and the ethics of knowing*. Oxford: Oxford University Press.

Grosfoguel, R. (2013). The structure of knowledge in westernised universities: Epistemic racism/sexism and the four genocides/epistemicides. *Human Architecture: Journal of the Sociology of Self-knowledge*, *1*(1), 73–90.

Hall, B. L., & Tandon, R. (2017). Decolonization of knowledge, epistemicide, participatory research and higher education. *Research for All*, *1*(1), 6–19.

Harber, C. (2019). *Schooling in sub-Saharan Africa: Policy, practice and patterns*. New York City: Guildford Press.

Hart, R. A. (1992). Children's participation: From tokenism to citizenship. UNICEF Innocenti Research Centre. Available at: https://www.unicef-irc.org/publications/100-childrens-participation-from-tokenism-to-citizenship.html [Retrieved: 6 March 2022].

Hill, L. (2014). 'Some of it I haven't told anybody else': Using photo elicitation to explore the experiences of secondary school education from the perspective of young people with a diagnosis of Autistic Spectrum Disorder. *Educational & Child Psychology, 31* (1), 79–89.

Hollway, W., & Jefferson, T. (2008). The free association narrative interview method. In L. M. Given (Ed.), *The SAGE encyclopedia of qualitative research methods* (pp. 296–315). Sevenoaks, CA: Sage.

Hollway, W., & Jefferson, T. (2012). *Doing qualitative research differently: A psychosocial approach.* London: Sage.

Holland, S., Renold, E., Ross, N. J., & Hillman, A. (2010). Power, agency and participatory agendas: A critical exploration of young people's engagement in participative qualitative research. *Childhood, 17*(3), 360–375.

James, A., & Prout, A. (2015). *Constructing and reconstructing childhood: contemporary issues in the sociological study of childhood.* London: Routledge.

Joffe, H., & Elsey, J. W. B. (2014). Free association in psychology and the grid elaboration method. *Review of General Psychology, 18*(3), 173–185.

Kellett, M. (2005). Children as active researchers: A new research paradigm for the 21st century. Economic and Social Research Council. Available at: http://oro.open.ac.uk/7539/ [Retrieved: 6 March 2022].

Lewis, A., Parsons, S., & Robertson, C. (2006). *My school, my family, my life: Telling it like it is.* Disability Rights Commission.

Mengwasser, E., & Walton, M. (2013). 'Show me what health means to you!' – Exploring children's perspectives of health. *Pastoral Care in Education, 31*(1), 4–14.

Mercieca, D., & Mercieca, D. P. (2014). EPs becoming ignorant: Questioning the assumption of listening and empowerment in young children. *Educational and Child Psychology, 31*(1), 22–31.

Messiou, K. (2002). Marginalisation in primary schools: Listening to children's voices. *Support for Learning, 17*(3), 117–121.

Moorosi, P., & Bush, T. (2020). *Development of School Leaders in Africa.* London: Bloomsbury Press.

Morrish, I. (2013). *Aspects of educational change.* London: Routledge.

Norwich, B., Kelly, N., & Educational Psychologists in Training. (2006). Evaluating children's participation in SEN procedures: Lessons for educational psychologists. *Educational Psychology in Practice, 22*(3), 255–271.

Office for National Statistics. (2020). Deaths involving COVID-19 by local area and socioeconomic deprivation: Deaths occurring between 1 March and 17 April 2020. Available at: https://www.ons .gov.uk/peoplepopulationandcommunity/birthsdeathsandmarriages/deaths/bulletins/deathsinvol vingcovid19bylocalareasanddeprivation/deathsoccurringbetween1marchand17april [Retrieved: 6 March 2022].

Park, J., & Mortell, J. (2020). Using the grid elaboration method (GEM) to investigate transition experiences of young autistic adults. *Educational Psychology in Practice, 36*(2), 193–207. https://doi .org/10.1080/02667363.2020.1731429

Possi, M. K., & Milinga, J. R. (2017). Special and inclusive education in Tanzania: Reminiscing the past, building the future. *Educational Process. International Journal, 6*(4), 55–73.

Pritchard, D. G. (1963). The development of schools for handicapped children in England during the nineteenth century. *History of Education Quarterly, 3*(4), 215–222.

Qvortrup, J. (1993). Societal position of childhood: The international project childhood as a social phenomenon. *Childhood, 1*(2), 119–124.

Sewell, A., & Smith, J. (2021). *Introduction to special educational needs, disability and inclusion: A student's guide.* London: SAGE.

Shepherd, J. (2015). Interviews: Listening to young people with autism in transition to college. *Exchanges: The Warwick Research Journal, 2*(2), 249–262.

Smillie, I. & Newton, M. (2020). Educational psychologists' practice: Obtaining and representing young people's views. *Educational Psychology in Practice, 36*(3), 328–344.

Sousa Santos, B. de (2007). Beyond abyssal thinking: From global lines to ecologies of knowledge. *Eurozine, 33*, 45–89.

Tams, C. (2018). Bye-bye, heroic leadership. Here comes shared leadership. *Forbes.* Available at: https://www.forbes.com/sites/carstentams/2018/03/09/bye-bye-heroic-leadership-here-comes -shared-leadership/?sh=3115f0b82c67 [Retrieved: 6 March 2022].

The Children's Act. (1989). Available at: https://www.legislation.gov.uk/ukpga/1989/41/contents [Retrieved: 3 November 2021].

UK Youth. (2020). *The impact of COVID-19 on young people and the youth sector.* Available at: https:// www.ukyouth.org/wp-content/uploads/2020/04/UK-Youth-Covid-19-Impact-Report-External -Final-08.04.20.pdf [Accessed: 6th March 2022].

Wallace, F., & Giles, P. (2019). Participatory research approaches in educational psychology training and practice. *Educational Psychology Research and Practice, 5*(1), 1–9.

Waller, T., & Bitou, A. (2011). Research with children: Three challenges for participatory research in early childhood. *European Early Childhood Education Research Journal, 19*(1), 5–20.

Warnock, M. (1978). Special educational needs: Report of the committee of enquiry into the education of handicapped children and young people. Available at: http://www.educationengland.org.uk/ documents/warnock/warnock1978.html [Retrieved: 31 January 2022].

Yahl, M. (2015). Education in Tanzania. New York University. Available at: https://pdf4pro.com/cdn/ education-in-tanzania-nyu-edu-5c2.pdf [Retrieved: 6 March 2022].

Chapter 6

VOICE PRACTICES TO SUPPORT PUPILS FROM THE GLOBAL MAJORITY

Maninder Kaur Sangar and Alexandra Sewell

Introduction

This chapter will:

- Consider how you can sensitively and meaningfully understand the voices of pupils who belong to the Global Majority.

- Provide a critical perspective on voice practices with pupils from the Global Majority.

- Discuss how the perspectives and opinions of Global Majority pupils can be listened to using approaches from narrative psychology and restorative practice.

Considering the Global Majority

The United Kingdom (UK) is ethnically and culturally diverse. There is increased attention on how the UK education system needs to reflect and respect the diversity of its pupils (Knowles & Lander, 2011). This too is true in the domain of meaningful voice practices. Informed and conscientious consideration needs to be given to the range of cultural experiences students from diverse backgrounds have and their unique right to a voice.

A key message of this chapter is that language matters. Terminology matters. As will be explored in depth in the section titled "Voice, knowledge, and language," language is the main mechanism through which both group and self-identity is created (Burr, 2015; Foucault, 1981). The "question of identity" (Hall, 2020, p. 42), and the role of language in this, has been argued to have increased importance in British cultural politics (Hall, 2020). Culturally, we are concerned with who we are as a nation and what it means to be "British." The understanding of race and ethnicity through terminology plays a significant part in this and cannot be ignored.

DOI: 10.4324/9781003165842-6

Black, Asian, and Minority Ethnic (BAME)

BAME (Black, Asian, and Minority Ethnic) is a term for referring to people of ethnicities which are not of Caucasian genetic lineage, and is well known and has been well used. It is an example of how language can create and reinforce non-inclusive constructions of ethnicity and identity. For example, it creates a perspective "that 'non-White' groups [are] much less differentiated than the term implies" (DaCosta, Dixon-Smith, & Singh, 2021). This hegemonic effect has real-world implications. For example, it creates an ill-defined concept for data collection and analysis in educational settings. Consider how data on educational attainment for students categorised as BAME obscures the relative performance of particular ethnic identities, such as the particular academic performance of Asian students at the A-level and higher education level compared to Black or White students (see Thiele, Singleton, Pope, & Stanistreet, 2016).

For these reasons, the dominance of the BAME conceptualisation of ethnic minorities ("minority" from a UK perspective) is diminishing. The UK government (2021) stated:

> We do not use the terms BAME (black, Asian and minority ethnic) and BME (black and minority ethnic) because they emphasise certain ethnic minority groups (Asian and Black) and exclude others (mixed, other and White ethnic minority groups). The terms can also mask disparities between different ethnic groups and create misleading interpretations of data.

This is a prescient example of how the role of language in the question of identity in British cultural politics should be paid close attention. We have sought to be reflexive in the writing of this chapter and so too have considered the terminology we use. We agree with the general trend away from BAME and the reasons for this. After joint reflection and discussion, we agreed on the term *Global Majority/Global Ethnic Majorities* (GM), whilst also referring "to ethnic minority groups individually, rather than as a single group" (UK Government, 2021). The term GM also enabled us to identify the intersubjectiveness of the language terms "majority" and "minority" (Campbell-Stephens, 2020). Britain's who wouldn't identify their ethnicity as "White" can also be constructed as a group from a global perspective. This positions such groups and individuals on a global stage, hopefully moving from lack of power as a minority to pointing out potential power as a majority (Campbell-Stephens, 2020).

Unique perspectives

Pupils who belong to the GM group have distinct perspectives and experiences. The concept of positionality refers to where we stand within a particular social, political, cultural context. It recognises the intersections of our race, class, gender, sexual orientation, religion, sexual orientation, immigration status, and so on. With positionality comes the concept of intersectionality, this is the "lens through which you can see where power comes and collides, where it interlocks and intersects" (Crenshaw, 2020). Our positionality and the concept of intersectionality produce unique systems of oppression and privilege. In order to grow our voice practice, we will need to consider our own positionalities and those of the individuals with whom we are engaging in order to authentically gather voice.

Reflective activity

Consider how you self-identify, your own ethnicity. What preferred language emerges? You may wish to mind-map any relations between terms and real world impacts in the space provided in Figure 6.1.

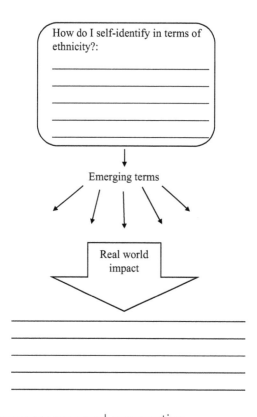

Figure 6.1 Ethnicity and language: personal perspective.

What terms have you experienced when being identified and constructed by others? You may wish to mind-map any relations between terms and real-world impacts in the space provided in Figure 6.2.

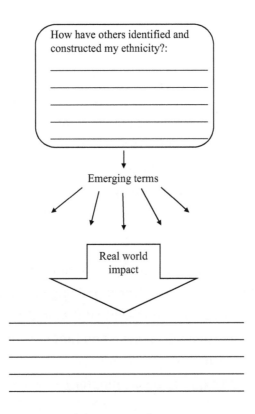

Figure 6.2 Ethnicity and language: social perspective.

Voice, knowledge, and language

As previously introduced, it is impossible to understand ethnicity and voice without exploring the role of language. In this section you are introduced to some key philosophical theory relating to the role of language in voice, and the influence of this in meaningful voice practices for GM pupils.

Language and voice

The production of voice often happens within a social space between two people (or groups of people) (Harcourt & Einarsdottir, 2011, p. 303). Language, although not the sole vehicle to produce voice, is the common means through which perspectives are shared and meaning comes into existence. Social constructionism views there to be multiple versions of reality or knowledge constructed within sociocultural, historical contexts. It therefore acknowledges positionality and the intersection of identities. Within this philosophical paradigm, language is viewed as constitutive and holding constructive power. Burr (2015) proposes that language and thoughts are inseparable: "Language provides the basis for all our thought" (p. 71).

Language therefore provides a structure to our experiences and gives it meaning. Meaning is co-constructed through dialogue. It is the site where we construct and reconstruct our identities. The meanings constructed through language shift depending on the context, time, and the people within that social interaction. This results in language becoming a site of conflict where power relations are enacted and contested (Burr, 2015; Foucault, 1977). We can see examples of this when we consider the discourses surrounding race. We find that racialised groups are often "othered" and constructed within marginalised and stereotypical narratives. Reassuringly, language also provides an opportunity for resistance and for reconstruction if we centre the voices of people from GM groups.

Bhopal (2018) outlines a pertinent example of how White speakers can produce a forceful collective voice through a sociocultural policing of what is deemed appropriate and inappropriate racial language use. It is argued that in the UK "a new racism has emerged in which appropriate racial discourse and language is used and is acceptable" (Bhopal, 2018, p. 24). This is termed *racetalk* and occurs when individuals with White privilege engage their voice to express discriminatory views towards an ethnic group but couch these views in language that they argue is not racist. For example, a White head teacher may state, "I disagree with affirmative action for ethnic minority educators as it means all employees are not judged on ability and performance." This statement does not use language terms and phrases traditionally judged to be racist. However, it serves to maintain White privilege by denying the extent of disadvantage for GM groups and ignoring systemic advantages that accompany being White.

Reflective activity

Danisha is 13 years old and has Afro-Caribbean heritage. During a physical education lesson, her team is losing a game of rounders. Danisha is upset about this. She waves the rounders bat towards her team members, raises her voice shouting, "Come on!! Why aren't you running fast enough! Move!"

With Danisha's Afro-Caribbean heritage in mind, what are the possible ways in which she may be constructed in relation to her voice in this scenario?

Discourses, power, objects, and subject positions

There are many definitions of what constitutes discourse. One definition describes discourses as "a set of meanings, metaphors, representations, images, stories, statements … that in some way together produce a particular version of events" (Burr, 2003, p. 64).

Discourses not only have the power to construct objects (things within a society) but also subjects (people) and subject positions. Taken together, if we consider that within a social interaction, depending on the positionality of the two people engaging in talk, the dialogue can produce power relations which in turn position the individuals (the subjects) in ways which has implications for the voice produced.

The French philosopher Michel Foucault (1981, p. 52) asserts that "in every society the production of discourse is at once controlled, selected, organized and redistributed by a certain number of procedures whose role is to ward off its powers and dangers." Foucault discusses how marginalised voices are often restricted, silenced, and excluded in order to perpetuate the dominant narrative within a society and maintain the status quo of oppression of people from the GM.

Individuals do of course have agency to accept or reject these subject positions. However, this is made challenging by the dominant discourses within a society and the availability of alternative discourses, which may constrain the possibilities of "being" in a range of ways. What follows is the importance of creating spaces where people from GM groups can self-define their identities and be collaborative meaning-makers to enable their unique voices to be truly included and heard.

Reflective activity

Within education which ethnic group's voices are privileged within the curriculum?

What are the implications of the presence of these voices for pupils from GM?

A critical perspective on voice practices with pupils from the Global Majority

When we begin to consider how we create voice spaces where pupils from the GM can self-define their identities, the critical question arises of how this is achieved in a meaningful, progressive way that does not fall prey to existing biases and assumptions. An oversimplified argument that is often made is that historically, educational research and practice concerning pupils from the GM has been done "to" rather than "with" them, and their voices have been absent. For example, Bagley (1972) conducted a study comparing the so-called deviant behaviour of English and West Indian "immigrant school children" (p. 47). The research method separated children by ethnicity and gender, and concluded that significantly more West Indian children were "disobedient" in a school setting. The positivist/quantitative paradigm for the research did not allow any space for understanding the perceptions and opinions of the participating children on their ostensible "disobedient behaviour" (p. 47). It also did not involve a reflection on existing assumptions and prejudices held by the researcher that may have influenced findings. As such, the line of argument follows that to therefore engage in meaningful voice practices we need to move towards doing "with."

This oversimplified debate is arguably misleading, as it is not reflexive practice to simply assume that moving towards doing "with" is liberational. De Palma (2008) argues that the inclusion of a diverse range of voices in the discussion of educational concerns alone is not sufficient. It is the nature of the discussion itself that requires critique. Within common discussion and speech about educational and pedagogic concerns, Whiteness is seen as default and therefore the "minority" is defined against the standards and values of the predominantly White space and often labelled as the "other." Individuals from the Global Majority therefore become the minority, the other, and subject of scrutiny to be measured, judged, and normalised. De Palma (2008) argues that the object of scrutiny should be the social construct of Whiteness and what comes with this in terms of unique characteristics, behaviours, ways of expressing the self, and perspectives.

As such, the objective of creating space for meaningful voice practices with GM pupils requires a layered consideration of language, power, existing prejudices and assumptions, and an exploration of misconceptions. You have already spent some time considering your own self-identity and use of language, and exploring how language can construct an individual's identity and position them within power relations. Next we outline some common misconceptions of voice work with GM pupils and invite you to further reflect on the development of your own practice.

Common misconceptions
Individual minority voices are representative of the whole ethnic group

There can be an assumption that if we engage in voice work with pupils from an ethnic group we have improved our understanding of that group (De Palma, 2008). This stems from a more fundamental assumption that identified ethnic groups are homogeneous when they are not. Whilst you may well be keen to address educational inequalities through voice practices with GM pupils, always consider that all pupil voice work is ultimately about attempting to diversify understanding through the nuance that arises from engaging individual perspectives.

If public discourse occurs, then diverse voices have been heard

Just because a social interaction has occurred within a voice project and lots of different individuals gave their views does not automatically mean that ethnically diverse voices have been heard, understood, and responded to in a meaningful way. For example, Lukšík (2019) found that the perspectives of Roma parents were not heard in public discourse. Eigenberg and Park (2016) examined 23 textbooks between 2008 and 2012 in relation to the intersections of race and gender. They found that the images reinforced stereotypes of White men as professionals, White women as victims, and Black males as victims. Women of colour remained invisible. This is evidence that there is a hierarchy of who is visible and whose views get paid heed to. As such, GM voice practices in educational contexts need to be cognisant of not just inviting dialogue but ensuring that it is a meaningful activity (see Chapter 1).

Engaging in voice activities will be enjoyable and liberating for Global Majority pupils

The enactment of voice practices for GM pupils by educational professionals often comes from a well-meaning place. Keen to promote equality and diversity in their educational setting, teachers and other key members of staff assume that GM pupils will openly welcome the voice work project, will enjoy it, and will feel liberated as a result. Firstly, as with all meaningful voice work, it should not be assumed that the target population will be interested and welcome this type of invitation. In any system that holds the value of democracy, non-participation is an act of agency and voice, as it gives a clear indication as to someone's opinion on whether they even wish to partake in discourse and debate. As such, GM pupils should never be co-opted into such activities.

Secondly, having to speak on behalf of the ethnic group you belong to and share experiences of racism is an emotional endeavour that can even be re-traumatising for individuals. As such, it is unlikely to be an enjoyable experience, even if it is viewed as worthwhile by participants. Such engagement in discourses for the betterment of society can be viewed as a form of emotional labour. Emotional labour is the expectation that individuals will manage their feelings in line with organisational rules (Wharton, 2009). In a GM pupil voice context this would be the expectation that although sharing complex emotional experiences, pupils should still manage behaviour and emotional expression to comply with school rules. They are being required to express verbally but not emote, which is a challenging experience.

Lastly, whilst it is hopeful that voice work practices with GM pupils will go some way to addressing inequalities and power imbalances in the education system, it is naïve to believe that they will be wonderfully transformative. If those in leadership positions in a school are White, this type of view can be interpreted as a manifestation of the white saviour complex (Aronson, 2017). Aronson (2017) defines white teacher saviourism as a teacher narrative born from adoption of a white saviour complex, where through interaction with GM pupils the White teacher believes their teaching is a heroic act, rewarding themselves for "saving" those less fortunate, whilst ignoring their privilege and Western policies that create and maintain oppression of GM.

Colour blindness

A final misconception is that race doesn't matter, or that a White teacher can best be inclusive by claiming "not to see colour." This is often apparent in comments such as "I treat all my students the same and don't notice their ethnicity" and "it doesn't matter what ethnicity a pupil is." This is termed colour blindness and occurs when a person believes that not noticing, or claiming not to notice, race and ethnicity can negate racial bias, prejudices, and racism (Younis & Jadhav, 2019). This perspective is a form of White privilege as it, again, involves ignoring and dismissing the existing social, political, and economic advantages White people have (Winter, Heath-Kelly, Kaleem, & Mills, 2022). It can also serve to silence the voice of GM pupils, as their existence and lived experience is unacknowledged. Instead, Winter et al. (2022) argue that Whiteness as the "default setting" (Winter et al., 2022, p. 88) needs to be challenged and the policy structures in school (such as the British values curriculum and Prevent strategy) that silence GM voices need to be challenged and overhauled as a sweeping and comprehensive act of meaningful voice practice.

Reflective activity

These common misconceptions often spark intense debate amongst educators. It is possible that at least one of the perspectives challenged your existing beliefs. The purpose of the reflective activity in Figure 6.3 is to help you to think through and challenge your initial reactions and to develop new perspectives as a result. For each misconception there is a seesaw to represent that such discussions can be polarising. Explore your initial reactions as a means to finding balance in the development of your personal stance.

'Minority voices are representative of the whole ethnic group'

What did I instinctively
disagree with?

_____
_____
_____
_____
_____
_____
_____

What did I instinctively
agree with?

_____
_____
_____
_____
_____
_____
_____

'If public discourse occurs, then diverse voices have been heard'

What did I instinctively
disagree with?

_____
_____
_____
_____
_____
_____
_____

What did I instinctively
agree with?

_____
_____
_____
_____
_____
_____
_____

'Engaging in voice activities will be enjoyable and liberational for GEM pupils'

What did I instinctively
disagree with?

_____
_____
_____
_____
_____
_____
_____
_____

What did I instinctively
agree with?

_____
_____
_____
_____
_____
_____

Colourblindness

What did I instinctively
disagree with?

_____
_____
_____
_____
_____
_____
_____

What did I instinctively
agree with?

_____
_____
_____
_____
_____

Figure 6.3 Challenging initial reactions.

Focus theory: The use of narrative psychological approaches to enhance voice practices with pupils from the GM

If I were to ask you the simple question of "tell me about yourself" you would likely respond by sharing some basic information such as your age, where you live, and what you do for work. If I pushed you further and asked "tell me more, tell me about who you *really* are," it would be likely that you would respond by telling me a story about who you are. This would not be too surprising. When asked about themselves in this way, people typically respond by forming a narrative of their life. Their story has a beginning point, something significant from their early childhood that is viewed as formative in creating who they are (Adler, Skalina, & McAdams, 2008). Their story has a middle which follows the literary device of conflict, such as a challenge they faced in becoming who they are (McAdams, 2008a). They typically draw a conclusion too, outlining how their story results in who they are now (McAdams, 2008a, 2008b).

Narrative psychology approaches are interested in these stories that people tell about themselves. The type of self-story outlined in the previous paragraph is viewed as a form of identity production. It is through the production of such narratives that we create and re-create who we view ourselves to be; our personalities and the meaning we give to our actions and the events in our lives (Vassilieva, 2016). McAdams (1994, p. 365, as cited in Vassilieva, 2016) refers to this as an individual's "vitalising life myth." What we say about ourselves is our "truth," a self-mythology that gives particular meaning to a person's life and is therefore a form of individual knowledge construction. The critical point of discussion here is not whether our story, or self/"life" myth, is actually true, but that once constructed it becomes a perspective we believe about ourselves, having impact on our personal psychology and how we live our lives.

Therefore, narrative psychological approaches provide a powerful way of exploring voice with pupils from GM backgrounds. They allow a child or young person to share their own self-story and how they view who they are; as within a story, events unfold in relation to the interpretations, thoughts, feelings, and beliefs of the narrator (Bruner, 1986; White & Epston, 1990 p. 123). An important caveat to this, however, is that although a story communicates an individual's views in a way that can be understandable to others, it does not give "direct access to experience: stories do not function as a 'mirror for life'" (White & Epston, 1990, p. 123). We must not mistake hearing about lived experience with the actuality of living events within a personal life story. When we are listening to stories we are therefore listening to the sense-making that an individual has of life events.

Narrative as a process

White and Epston (1990, 1992) developed narrative therapy, as they believed that storytelling is a powerful way for humans to process and understand their experiences. This is what is known as narrative-as-process. Similar to the work of McAdams (2008a, 2008b), narrative-as-process is a route for an individual to create and sustain a preferred sense of self. In essence, it is the supporting of a person to identify their self-narrative, and understand their values, actions, and how they live out their stories (White & Epston, 1990). Our lives are viewed as being multi-storied. In a therapeutic context, this approach is used to help a person understand problems faced in their life and to generate preferred stories that are hopeful and linked with the person that they want to become (Matos, Santos, Gonçalves, & Martins, 2009; White & Epston, 1992).

Stories that we construct about ourselves and others are linked with wider cultural discourses (e.g. race, gender, sexuality). By adopting a narrative approach, we can decentre ourselves and the cultural biases, interpretations, and positions we hold which impact our story-making about ourselves and others in relation to us. Narrative-as-process has also been of increasing interest in educational contexts to help pupils understand and share their sense of self through self-story creation, and to identify and find resolutions to problems arising in learning settings (Romagnolo & Ohrt, 2017).

Externalisation

One approach within narrative-as-process is externalisation. Externalisation involves an attempt to identify and characterise a problem or event that has impacted a person and place it outside of the self to objectify the lived experience (Matos et al., 2009). Through externalisation the problem or event becomes a separate entity to the person so it can be viewed from a distanced, nuanced perspective. This opens possibilities for a non-judgemental conversation about the person's position on the problem, the effects of the problem, and actions they might take to overcome the problem. It also opens dialogue about how problems link with dominant cultural perspectives. If these are identified with, they are kept. Otherwise, they are discarded, and the process thus offers "the provision of space for the performance of alternative, previously neglected or subjugated knowledges" (Vassilieva, 2016, p. 32).

As such, narrative therapy and the externalisation process seeks to challenge how marginalised voices, such as those of GM pupils, are silenced through the perpetuation and adoption of dominant narratives in society (Foucault, 1981, p. 52). Externalisation can provide a route for extraction of ideological positions that may have negatively influenced people from GMs' personal narrative creation, and thus reveal alternative (often termed "indigenous" or "folk") ways of knowing. Through this process, meaningful voice work can occur.

Externalisation examples from Maninder Sangar's research

Maninder Kaur Sangar

Within my doctoral research, I explored the voice of secondary school-level South Asian girls in relation to the concepts of "mental health" and "shame." Externalisation was used as a tool to deconstruct the South Asian girls' constructions of these concepts. As part of the externalisation process, the participants were asked to imagine the concepts of mental health and shame as living beings or objects. They were asked to characterise these objects, to imagine them sitting in the room. I asked externalising questions such as:

- What did shame and mental health look like?
- What actions did they undertake?
- What would they say if they could speak?
- What impact would they have? (Sangar, 2018)

Externalisation questions allow us to open possibilities and create meaning about concepts which are complex and not easily understood. It allows nuanced meanings to be made which may or may not align with wider discourses within society. The consequence of this line of enquiry was that the girls produced rich, nuanced, and detailed stories about mental health and shame, which provided unique meanings. The process of externalisation centred the participants' sense-making and provided a playful way to explore the phenomena, opening alternative discourses and creating space for authentic voice practice.

Following are examples of voices of South Asian girls in relation to mental health and shame when they were asked the externalising questions shared earlier.

Externalised constructions of mental health (Sangar, 2018):

ok I've drawn a brain and then all of these things symbolise Mental Health because ... if you have like a nice normal brain, it's almost like a disease like there's something infecting it, it hurts, hence the sharp bits and not like everyone will be able to realise that because it's not like physical pain, it's different for everyone ... they're like mental illness jabbing into you ... it hurts

it's meant to be this box with a key hole and there's a heart that's broken, for me I feel like when I think of mental health I think of something that's closed off, you're keeping to yourself and its locked away

Externalised constructions of shame (Sangar, 2018):

Shame would be like the internet, or the computer or your phone ... because we have the media, we have the internet, it's so wide, and we learn so much from it, it's bad or good and Shame comes through so many forms

it's a wooden cube I think it would show like different scenarios like each side it has erm there's like say there's culture, and erm religion, like it could have different like pictures kind of ... they'd just be walking and showing them the different ways a person can be, yeah, it's showing them different ways a person can be ... say if it was a relationship, it will show you the good side of it and then it will show you the bad side of it, and then it would show you the culture side of it and then the religion side of it, all the sides and then at the end you will, you will pick one. ... say if you did it like this way what would happen and if you did it that way what would happen as well.

What I hope you will notice is that the examples show that there are multiple ways of talking about mental health and shame. There are no right or wrong definitions, as each is the individual's sense-making. Each description can therefore coexist as competing discourses within society. This is important when working with GM, as the ways in which social constructs come to be defined are culturally, socially, historically, and contextually located. There are multiple ways in which cultures make sense of ideas such as mental health and shame. When enacting authentic voice practice with individuals from the GM what we are endeavouring to do is to open up talk around concepts and to surface the multitude of ideas around them without placing judgment on what we consider to be correct or incorrect.

Reflective activity

Consider a social construct that you are interested in obtaining GM children's views about (e.g. race, gender, family, childhood).

Imagine this construct as a living being or object. Consider the following externalising questions that Sangar (2018) used in her research:

- What would it look like?

- What would it do?

- If it could speak what would it say?

- What impact would it have?

How can these externalising questions be used to enhance your voice practice with GM pupils?

Practice focus: Relational practice – A vehicle towards restorative justice

Friere (1970) argues the importance of humility, love, faith, hope, and critical thinking as key considerations for effective dialogue. If we take what we have discussed so far, everyone embodies a unique positionality. With this comes sites of oppression and privilege, usually perpetuating harm for individuals from GM. To grow our awareness of these factors and to establish a levelling of power dynamics we will need to confront them with said humility, love, faith, hope, and critical thinking.

Vaandering (2013) proposes a way to do this using the relationship window. This framework enables us to reflect on our interpersonal interactions with others and to consider whether we are causing harm in those interactions. The underpinning philosophy behind this framework is that all human beings are worthy of being honoured and valued. Figure 6.4 displays the relationship window and how this applies to voice practice.

If we are operating within the quadrants of To, Not, and For, it is likely we are perpetuating harm to another. If we are able to relate with others as humans, particularly with those who belong to GM (who are often dehumanised or othered), in an honourable way, having high expectations and high levels of support, we are more able to produce authentic voice practice.

Reflective activity

In Figure 6.5, list the common phrases/statements/questions that you use in your teaching practice with children to assert authority.

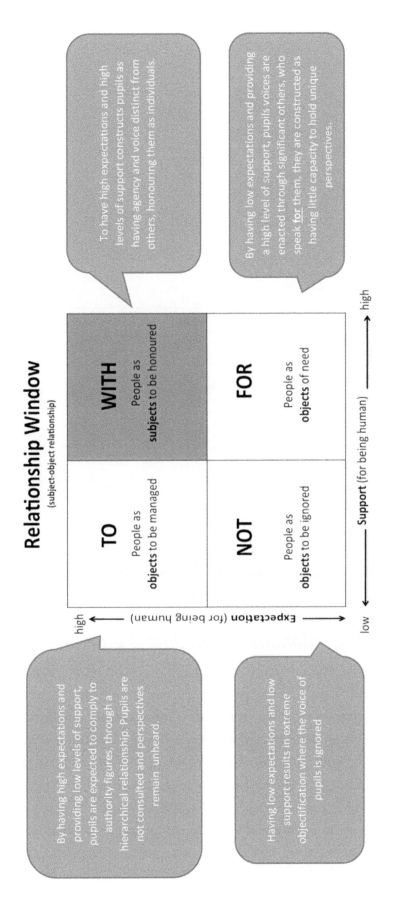

Figure 6.4

_____

_____

_____

_____

Sort the statements under the following headings:

TO	WITH
NOT	FOR

Figure 6.5 Applying the relationships window.

On reviewing this task, are you working in an honourable way with GM pupils, viewing them as equals?

Example of how the relationship window is enacted

There are many incidents that happen within educational settings where harm has occurred between two people, e.g. bullying, fights, name-calling. When this happens, educators have a choice to operate in either one of the quadrants described in Vaandering's (2013) relationship window. In order to operate within the With quadrant, where we are honouring each individual as human subjects, we can use tools from restorative practice. One tool, called mediation or short conference, is helpful to ensure voices are heard from both parties. The purpose of mediation is to bring people together when harm has occurred, to enable them to explore the incident, what needs to happen to restore a relationship, and to come to a shared agreement about how they would like to move forward.

Figure 6.6 shows a series of stages that can be followed to enable each person's voice to be shared within a mediation session (adapted from Newton & Mahaffey, 2008).

1) **Welcome and opening**	Introductions of participants (the adult dealing with the incident and the individuals involved). A context is set for listening and sharing Ground rules are agreed (including time out) to establish safety
2) **Exploration (past/present)**	The stories of the incident are explored: What has happened, What the individuals were thinking, What they were feeling Who has been affected, What has happened since Each participant is asked questions in turn before moving onto the next stage.
3) **Moving on (present/future)**	Check what the individuals need now and next to restore things. The individuals are invited to say something in response to what they have heard from one another.
4) **Negotiating agreements**	Invitations to share what might need to happen next to repair the harm are shared. Pupils and participants are encouraged to take the lead in negotiating. Pupils can do this together on their own and bring back to share if they choose. How might the child begin to put things right/make amends/ repair the relationship?
5) **Closure**	The facilitator draws together what has been achieved by everyone in the meeting. Part of this phase includes reminders of follow up actions.

Figure 6.6 Mediation session structure.

The structure provides an opportunity for each individual's voice to be heard in a safe and contained manner. It enables each person to be treated with dignity, respect, and humanity. We can prevent ourselves from falling into the trap of assumptions and judgments about what we think may have happened or needs to happen as a course of action following an incident. It enables the individuals' voices to be heard, to come to a shared understanding of what has happened and an opportunity to rebuild relationships which may have been damaged by the incident.

Reflective activity

Consider a group of children or staff who would benefit from a mediation session as outlined in the previous section. Use Figure 6.6 to plan the session and, if it feels appropriate, try it out.

Chapter summary

In this chapter we have attempted not just to offer theoretical and practice foci for developing your voice practice with GM pupils but also offer a critical perspective on engagement with these voice practices. Before embarking on meaningful voice practices for GM pupils, an orientation to how language (inherent in voice) positions individuals with respect to ethnicity and creates discrepancies in power dynamics is important. Narrative psychological approaches offer the tool of narrative-as-process, whereby the viewpoints of GM pupils can be externalised, viewed with some distance, and transformed – if wished. Restorative practice techniques offer a means for providing a space for the voice of GM pupils in a humanising way.

Action plan

PLAN			
ETHOS How do you currently engage and support the voices of Global Ethnic Majority pupils in your school? How effective is this? What needs to change?		**GOALS** What do you want to achieve?	
DO			
TASKS Break your goal into discrete tasks to be completed	**TIME LIMITS** Set a realistic time for your tasks to be completed by	**RESOURCES / ACTIONS / ACTIVITIES** What resources will you use? Who is responsible for doing what?	**COMPLETED** Tick this box when each task has been achieved.
REVIEW			
WHAT WENT WELL?	**WHAT WOULD YOU DO DIFFERENTLY?**	**WHAT ARE YOUR ONGOING PLANS FOR DEVELOPING GLOBAL ETHNIC MAJORITY VOICE PRACTICES?**	

Figure 6.7 Supporting the voices of pupils from the Global Majority action plan.

Further reading

White Privilege: The Myth of a Post Racial Society by Kalwant Bhopal – This book provides a detailed analysis of how racism and White privilege continue to negatively shape the British education system and the impact this has on children and young people. It makes a poignant application of neoliberalism and critical race theory to expand on difficulties encountered in the current schooling context.

Why I'm No Longer Talking to White People About Race by Reni Eddo-Lodge – Whilst this book does not primarily concentrate on education, it is a key read for developing one's understanding about the history of voice oppression GM individuals have experienced. It also provides a contemporary analysis of how GM voices and perspectives continue to be subjugated.

References

Adler, J. M., Skalina, L. M., & McAdams, D. P. (2008). The narrative reconstruction of psychotherapy and psychological health. *Psychotherapy Research*, *18*(6), 719–734.

Aronson, B. A. (2017). The white savior industrial complex: A cultural studies analysis of a teacher educator, savior film, and future teachers. *Journal of Critical Thought and Praxis*, *6*(3), 36–54.

Bagley, C. (1972). Deviant behaviour in English and West Indian schoolchildren. *Research in Education*, *8*(1), 47–55.

Bhopal, K. (2018). *White privilege: The myth of a post-racial society*. London: Policy Press.

Bruner, E. M. (1986). *The anthropology of experience*. Chicago: University of Illinois Press.

Burr, V. (2003). *Social constructionism* (2nd edn). London: Routledge.

Burr, V. (2015). *Social constructionism*. London: Routledge.

Campbell-Stephens, R. (2020). *Global Majority: Decolonising the language and Reframing the Conversation about Race*. Leeds Beckett University. Available at: https://www.leedsbeckett.ac.uk/-/media/files/schools/school-of-education/final-leeds-beckett-1102-global-majority-9221.docx#:~:text=Global%20Majority%20is%20a%20collective,racialised%20as%20'ethnic%20minorities' [Retrieved: 14 March 2022].

Crenshaw, K. (2020). *Intersectionality*. Available at: https://time.com/5786710/kimberle-crenshaw-intersectionality/ [Retrieved: 14 March 2022].

DaCosta, C., Dixon-Smith, S., & Singh, G. (2021). *Beyond BAME: Rethinking the politics, construction, application and efficacy of ethnic categorization*. Higher Education Research Action Group (HERAG). Available at: https://pure.coventry.ac.uk/ws/portalfiles/portal/41898015/Beyond_BAME_final_report.pdf [Retrieved: 11 March 2022].

DePalma, R. (2008). "The voice of every Black person"?: Bringing authentic minority voices into the multicultural dialogue. *Teaching and Teacher Education*, *24*(3), 767–778.

Eigenberg, H. M., & Min Park, S. (2016). Marginalization and invisibility of women of color: A content analysis of race and gender images in introductory criminal justice and criminology texts. *Race and Justice*, *6*(3), 257–279.

Foucault, M. (1977). *Discipline and punish: The birth of the prison*. London: Penguin.

Foucault, M. (1981). The order of discourse. In R. Young (Ed.), *Untying the text: A poststructuralist reader*. London: Routledge.

Friere, P. (1970). *Pedagogy of the oppressed*. New York: Continuum.

Hall, S. (2020). Old and new identities, old and new ethnicities. In L. Back & J. Solomos (Eds.), *Theories of race and racism: A Reader*. London: Routledge.

Harcourt, D., & Einarsdóttir, J. (2011). Introducing children's perspectives and participation in research. *European Early Childhood Education Research Journal, 19*(3), 301–307.

Holstein, J., & Gubrium, J. (1995). *The active interview.* London: Sage.

Hopkins, B. (1999). *The restorative classroom: Using restorative approaches to foster effective learning.* London: Optimus Education: A Division of Optimus Professional Publishing Ltd.

Hopkins, B. (2015). *Restorative theory in practice: Insights into what works and why.* London: Jessica Kingsley Publishers.

https://publications.parliament.uk/pa/cm201617/cmselect/cmhealth/849/84902.htm [Retrieved: March 2017].

Knowles, G., & Lander, V. (2011). *Diversity, equality and achievement in education.* London: Sage Publications.

Lukšík, I. (2019). Children from marginalised Roma communities at the school gates: The disconnect between majority discourses and minority voices. *Early Childhood Education Journal, 47*(6), 665–675.

Mahaffey, H., & Newton, C. (2008). *Restorative solutions: Making it work, improving challenging behaviour and relationships in schools.* Nottingham: Inclusive Solutions UK Limited.

Matos, M., Santos, A., Gonçalves, M., & Martins, C. (2009). Innovative moments and change in narrative therapy. *Psychotherapy Research, 19*(1), 68–80.

McAdams, D. P. (1994). Can personality change? Levels of stability and change across the life span. In T. F. Heatherton, & J. L. Weinberger (Eds.), *Can personality change?* Washington: American Psychology Association.

McAdams, D. P. (2008a). *The person: An introduction to the science of personality psychology.* Hoboken: John Wiley & Sons.

McAdams, D. P. (2008b). Personal narratives and the life story. In O. P. John, R. W. Robins, & L. A. Pervin (Eds.), *Handbook of personality: Theory and research.* New York: Guilford Press.

Newton, C., & Mahaffey, H. (2008). *Restorative solutions: Making it work.* Nottingham: Inclusive Solutions UK Limited.

Romagnolo, S. M., & Ohrt, J. H. (2017). Using narrative therapy with low-income middle school students: A model for school counselors. *Journal of Child and Adolescent Counseling, 3*(1), 59–73.

Sangar, M. K. (2018). *Mental health and shame: A Foucauldian analysis of the discourses of South Asian girls and their teachers* (Doctoral dissertation, University of Birmingham).

Thiele, T., Singleton, A., Pope, D., & Stanistreet, D. (2016). Predicting students' academic performance based on school and socio-demographic characteristics. *Studies in Higher Education, 41*(8), 1424–1446.

UK Government. (2021). *Writing about ethnicity.* Available at: https://www.ethnicity-facts-figures.service.gov.uk/style-guide/writing-about-ethnicity#bame-and-bme [Retrieved: 1 March 2022].

Vaandering, D. (2013). A window on relationships: Reflecting critically on a current restorative justice theory. *Restorative Justice, 1*(3), 311–333.

Vassilieva, J. (2016). *Narrative psychology: Identity, transformation and ethics.* London: Springer.

Wharton, A. S. (2009). The sociology of emotional labor. *Annual Review of Sociology, 35*, 147–165.

White, M., & Epston, D. (1990). *Narrative means to therapeutic ends*. New York: Norton.

White, M., & Epston, D. (1992). *Experience, contradiction, narrative and imagination* (2nd ed.). Adelaide, South Australia: Dulwich Centre Publications.

Winter, C., Heath-Kelly, C., Kaleem, A., & Mills, C. (2022). A moral education? British values, colour-blindness, and preventing terrorism. *Critical Social Policy*, *42*(1), 85–106.

Younis, T., & Jadhav, S. (2019). Keeping our mouths shut: The fear and racialized self-censorship of British healthcare professionals in Prevent training. *Culture, Medicine and Psychiatry*, *43*(3), 404–424.

Chapter 7

VOICE PRACTICES TO SUPPORT PUPILS OF DIVERSE GENDERS

Anastasia Kennett, Max Davies, and Alexandra Sewell

Introduction

This chapter will:

- Offer a progressive understanding of gender by outlining key concepts and theory.

- Introduce gender-creative parenting as a model that can be applied in educational contexts to create a systemic approach for meaningful voice practices concerned with gender identity.

- Explore practical school-based strategies for enhancing voice practices supporting pupils of diverse genders and support you to reflect on how these might be useful in your setting.

A progressive understanding of gender

In this chapter we first outline key concepts of sex, gender, and cisgender. We then discuss key theories which explain how children come to understand gender and self-identify their own gender. The perspective of gender-creative parenting is then presented as a progressive way to conceptualise gender and to be with children with a sensitive regard to their gender development. Following this, we critically explore pupil voice to support pupils of diverse genders with practice examples and reflective activities to help you develop your own positioning on the topic and associated educational voice practice.

Key concepts

Sex

West and Zimmerman (1991, p. 13) describe sex as "abscribed by biology: anatomy, hormones, and physiology." From a traditional medical perspective two dichotomous sexes have been identified. These are male and female. Children are assigned their sex at birth.

DOI: 10.4324/9781003165842-7

This is predominantly based on visual anatomy, although other determining factors can also be used. This is known as their anatomical sex (see Genderbread Person, 2022).

However, a different perspective on sex can also be adopted as variations in visual anatomy, as well as in hormones and physiology, can occur. People are born with sexual and reproductive anatomy that is not consistent with a "typical idea of the 'sexual dimorphism of male/female'" (Barker & Iantaffi, 2019, p. 57) known as "intersex." Barker and Iantaffi (2019) state that as the labelling of one's anatomical sex is derived from visual anatomy rather than any other determining factor, some children's chromosomal makeup goes unanalysed. From this perspective, the idea of the two male and female sexes is viewed as simplistic, and the notion of a spectrum of anatomical and biological sex has been made (Ainsworth, 2015). There is therefore continuing debate as to whether anatomical sex should be considered binary or a spectrum. We make no claims for either here but present both ideas to demonstrate current cultural and scientific discussions on the topic.

Gender

West and Zimmerman (1991) describe gender as "an achieved status: that which is constructed through psychological, cultural, and social means" (p. 13). They speak of gender as a process of "doing" which can be considered a "performance" of specific acts concerning the social ideas of gender (Butler, 1988). It has been argued that historically "feminist scholars promoted the use of the term gender to draw attention to the reality that not all differences between men and women could be explained by biology" (Short, Yang, & Jenkins, 2013, p. 594).

The performance of gender involves the reproduction of gender stereotypes. These can begin at birth and be as simple as baby clothes, such as pretty pink bows for girls and blue trousers for boys. Gender stereotypes also indicate a set of behavioural expectations. For example, that boys enjoy rough and tumble play, and that girls are pleasant and compliant. Gender also comes with numerous expectations of what girls and boys can and can't do.

Cisgender and gender as a spectrum

Aultman (2014) defines cisgender as a term that "can be used to describe individuals who possess, from birth and into adulthood, the male or female reproductive organs (sex) typical of the social category of man or woman (gender) to which that individual was assigned at birth" (p. 61). When a body does not perform to a correct concept of gender, identities such as transgender, non-binary, and gender non-conforming start forming. For example, transgender is the opposite of cisgender, a person whose body (sex) does not align with their gender (performative acts). Transgender and intersex people "do" sex and gender differently and paradoxically construct new ideas of how we develop, experience, or perform gender.

Key theories
Social learning theory (Mischel, 1966)

Social learning theory is the concept of learning one's gender by sex-typed reinforcement through rewards and punishment from others in the developmental environment (Blakemore et al., 2009; Mischel, 1966). A child will receive different types of treatment because of their sex, motivating them to align themselves to the gender they've been assigned (Blakemore, Berenbaum, & Libe, 2009; Martin, Ruble, & Szkrybalo, 2002; Mischel, 1966; Josephidou & Bolshaw, 2020).

This is a complex and layered process. Children may structure sex-role concepts in line with given social-environmental expectations. However, no two adults are synchronised in every performative aspect of maleness and femaleness, resulting in children learning conflicting behaviours. It has been stated that "exposure to models of both sexes is sufficient for the child to acquire many responses from the repertoires of both sexes" (Mischel, 1966, p. 59). Therefore, many children perform behaviours deemed opposite-sex behaviour. It is "through observational learning boys and girls typically acquire many of the behaviours of both sexes," which will impact on their reward and punishment process as social agents attempting to continuously realign behaviours to their understanding of sex/gender and maleness/femaleness (Mischel, 1966, p. 59).

Cognitive developmental theory (Kholberg, 1966)

Kohlberg (1966) examined the cognitive-developmental process children undergo to attain knowledge and understanding of their gender identity (Blakemore et al., 2009; Martin et al., 2002; Mischel, 1966; Josephidou & Bolshaw, 2020). It is through many social learning examples that children develop cognitive gender schema. By the following ages children are typically able to do the following:

Age 2–3: Align with their gender identity through social performance.

Age 5–6: Consistently identify people by gender.

Age 7–8: Possess stability in gender identity and understanding.

Kohlberg (1966) argues that gender identity is neither purely biological nor social. It is the child's cognitive categorisation of what gender is and how it is accomplished that is the reason for their consistent performance of gender.

Reflective activity

Chose an age group to observe that aligns with Kohlberg's (1966) theory of gender schema development, i.e. 2–3 years old, 5–6 years old, 7–8 years old. If you do not have access to these age groups, you can observe older children. Spend half an hour watching them in a socially interactive environment. Pay note to what toys and activities children play with and how they play with them. Also, take an interest in how they communicate with each other. What behaviours do the children exhibit that portray a potential developmental understanding of gender expression cues and their own gender? Does this align with Kohlberg (1966), or do you observe something different?

Gender schema theory (Bem, 1981, 1983)

Bem (1981, 1983) draws together both social learning theory and cognitive developmental theory. We can see why Kolhberg (1966) argued that gender development is not entirely environmental, as there are a lot of inconsistencies in gender expressions and identities that are not an exact replication of what is being taught and learnt. Therefore, children interpret the information given and decide relevant and important information they would seek and maintain regarding gender and their gender identity. For this reason, Bem's gender schema theory (1983, 1981) is apt, as it suggests a child's developmental understanding of gender "derives largely from gender-schematic processing" (Bem, 1983, p. 603). Bem (1983, p. 603) believes that "sex typing is a learned phenomenon and, hence, that it is neither inevitable nor unmodifiable." Children being active participants learn direct gender responses or decode "omitting" behaviours.

Children's active role is obvious in their constructive information processing as well as in their motivation to adhere to gender-related behaviours. Schemas are not seen as passive copies of the environment; they are viewed as active constructions, prone to errors and distortions (Martin et al., 2002, p. 911). Research has found that children are able to replicate gendered information and performatively align with their assigned gender, even if they do not actively identify themselves as that gender (Bem, 1983; Davies, 2003; Josephidou & Bolshaw, 2020).

Reflective activity

Pearson (2021) explored gendered social constructions about masculinity in relation to boy's mental health in educational contexts. They put forth that a hegemonic construction of masculinity in Western society is characterised by "notions of emotional and physical strength and toughness, power and stoicism" (p. 2). The emotional strength and emotional inarticulation positioning of the male gender are hypothesised to restrict boy's ability to express emotions, leading to detrimental mental health (Pearson, 2021). Following are quotes from boys that Pearson (2021) interviewed (in Year 8 and Year 9) to explore how they adopted and constructed this gendered view of masculinity and emotion. Read the quotes and reflect on whether any dominant gendered narratives around how boys should be and act regarding emotional experiences are present. What impact could this have for boy's gender performance and developmental well-being?

Quote 1:

> It's where someone's really ... sort of a psycho, but, they need help, they, make other lives misery, other people's lives misery, they, something bad's probably ... someone's hurt them like say like, abuse ... that could make someone, really, not stable ... could have a mental breakdown.
>
> *(Pearson, 2021, p. 17)*

Notes on gendered perspective noticeable in the quote:

_____
_____
_____
_____

Figure 7.1 Notes.

Quote 2:

> [mental health is...] like they can't control themselves and like, isn't it like where you've like, nearly killed someone and then like you get put in a hos, mental health hospital?
>
> *(Pearson, 2021, p. 17)*

Notes on gendered perspective noticeable in the quote:

_____
_____
_____
_____

Figure 7.1 Notes.

Quote 3:

> I'm trying to ... listen to what people are saying, I can ignore them if they say it once, I can ignore them ... if you say it a few times so if they say it too many times I just hit them without thinking ... I lash out too much at people
>
> *(Pearson, 2021, p. 18)*

Notes on gendered perspective noticeable in the quote:

_____
_____
_____
_____

Figure 7.1 Notes.

Quote 4:

> I have had loads of fights ... I've just, said something that I didn't really mean, and other people have got involved and said hit him, hit him, hit him, and I've listened to them, without thinking

(Pearson, 2021, p. 15)

Notes on gendered perspective noticeable in the quote:

_____
_____
_____
_____

Figure 7.1 Notes.

Theoretical focus: A gender-creative perspective
Parenting models

A parenting model is a proactive approach to childhood development that is derived from psychological research that explores the impact of parenting style on the child. In the late 20th century parenting models emerged that sought to apply theory of gender development to parenting practices. Gender-creative parenting is a parenting model that developed because of these practices and which we position in this chapter as being one approach to apply for engaging in meaningful voice work practices that consider the complexities of gender development in children and young people.

Non-sexist childrearing

The influence of social learning theories led to a subsection of mothers in the 1970s and 1980s to apply the idea that gender is socialised through social models in the environment, and also via the schema children develop in relation to this. The aim was to encourage girls to renounce the stereotypical ideas of how they should perform their gender (Statham, 1986). This was termed non-sexist childrearing and encompassed how girls dressed, what toys they played with, and the playmates they had access to (Martin, 2005). Mothers also attempted to model this themselves (Martin, 2005). The aim was to promote movement towards a society where women were equal to men.

Gender-neutral parenting

Towards the end of the 1990s, gender-neutral parenting emerged as a new parenting model (Martin, 2005). The goal of gender-neutral parenting is to limit children's access to gendered information and gender stereotypes. For example, by making sure both girls and boys have access to a range of toys that are stereotypically considered the provenance of the opposite gender. There was an inclusion of the recognition of the effect of gendering on boys. Gender-neutral parenting still uses gender and sex markers, such as identifying the sex of a child and using corresponding sex-based pronouns. Children are still gendered but the influence of stereotypes in restricting the performative behavioural repertoire of each gender is managed.

Gender-creative parenting

Gender-creative parenting differs from gender-neutral parenting as a model as it seeks to challenge conceptions of sex as well as gender (Morris, 2018; Myers, 2020). For example, gender-neutral pronouns are used for a child from birth so as not to divide children into gender and sex categories. Children are also taught about anatomy but not as exclusively belonging to girl/boy genitalia to create an environment where children can feel comfortable to self-identify their gender. Using language and sex education in this way is viewed as using inclusive and neutral language that makes it possible for children and young people to identify as trans, gender non-conforming, or non-binary, if this feels right for them personally.

The gender-creative approach and meaningful voice practices

Is it our responsibility as adults to involve children in all areas of their lives. This includes the development of their gender identity. With regard to knowledge production in general, but specifically that relating to gender identity understanding and development in children and young people, this "immediately raises problems for children's voices because to have influence their voice must transcend the cultural boundaries of childhood and negotiate a shared understanding in the adult world" (Kellett, 2010, p. 196). A critical question is whether children and young people's views are given freedom of expression with respect to the genderisation of childhood and their attempt to develop a gender identity within this context.

A pertinent example is language used in the United Nations Convention on the Rights of the Child (UNCRC) (1989) (see Chapter 2). It explicitly states a child's right to express their views freely and have the ability to "seek, receive and impart information and ideas of all kinds ... either orally, in writing or in print, in the form of art, or through any other media of the child's choice'" (UNCRC, 1989, p. 5). However, with regard to gender diversity, the convention itself arguably does not meet this aim. The pronouns he/she are used consistently throughout. Article 17d stipulates that mass media dissemination should pay particular attention to the linguistic needs of children belonging to minority groups. Yet here it arguably fails to represent children who are gender creative, diverse, trans, or non-binary. It could be viewed as an anachronistic document that requires updating in line with contemporary views and associated language developments.

The concept of gender-neutral parenting would arguably be adaptable to educational contexts to create a systemic voice environment where those whose identity is at odds with dualistic notions of gender feel comfortable to express their views and perceptions, and have them responded to (Ferfolja & Ullman, 2021). Gender creativity as an approach is "the artistry we use to weave together a unique and authentic gender self, based on core feelings and chosen gender expression" (Ehrensaft, 2011, pp. 102–117). Weaving it into educational practice in this way would require practitioners to confront their own views of gender and gender construction, to develop new beliefs and values about gender (Bem, 1983, p. 610). The hope is that such an application of the gender-creative approach to educational contexts would give children more gender freedom. This would allow them to develop egalitarian views of gender and of what children can do throughout their lives (Risman & Myers, 1997).

An example of the application of the gender-creative approach to a school context is Egalia, a school in Sweden that practices gender-creative child rearing (Erdol, 2019). Egalia looks to leave gender behind, using neutral language towards the children, such as "friends," and deconstructing gender and gender roles in toys and educational materials. Children are allowed to play with whatever they chose and all toys are neutral in gender, including dolls. The pre-school curriculum asks practitioners to "counteract traditional gender patterns and gender roles" (Sandstrom, Steir, & Sandberg, 2013, p. 124). The gender-neutral pronoun of *hen* is applied to all children (Erdol, 2019).

Reflective activity

Gender-creative parenting and the application of its approach to educational contexts has been presented here as it provides a radical example for understanding and responding to gender diversity. As with every content chapter and reflective activity in this book, the aim is to present you with challenging ideas so that you can develop your own voice perspective on the matter and related meaningful voice practices. Radical examples naturally challenge our existing assumptions and therefore allow us to potentially begin to adopt new perspectives. You may not see yourself fully becoming a gender-creative educational practitioner, but you may wish to shift your thinking in some way. What has challenged you and potentially shifted in your thinking? If you were to select one aspect of the gender-creative approach to adopt as part of your voice practice, what would it be and why?

Practice focus: Strategies for enhancing voice practices to support pupils of diverse genders

There is a new recognition within education to increase the need for "spaces of agency, belonging and inclusion" for pupils with diverse genders (Reygan, 2019, p. 91). Pupils with diverse genders have tended to exhibit enhanced self-advocacy skills within schools because they are often responsible for replying to inappropriate questions and requesting gender equality and acceptance (Ferfolja & Ullman, 2021). This demonstrates an ability to have agency and power over their own lives via an effective utilisation of voice. However, not all pupils feel confident to engage in self-advocacy (Reygan, 2019). Therefore, schools cannot always rely on the child's ability to speak up about any potential changes that need to be made within the school culture. The following outlines many examples of how schools can facilitate an environment that is open and responsive to the voices of pupils from diverse genders.

Parents as a conduit for pupil voice

If pupils are finding engagement in self-advocacy to be a daunting task, an alternative approach could be to utilise the child's parents as spokespersons. Parents find that they are often needed to step into schools to advocate on behalf of their children regarding such things as bullying, exclusion, and the teaching methods/curriculum. This has often led to the schools acting on the parents' wishes (Davy & Cordoba, 2020; Ferfolja & Ullman, 2021). This demonstrates the extent to which "parents are beginning to enact cultural changes in schools regarding gender diversity and awareness" (Davy & Cordoba, 2020, p. 349). However, neither of these self-advocacy examples situate the child at the forefront of participatory methods (Hart, 1992). They do, however, provide an avenue in which the child's voice can be heard by teachers.

Yet when teachers are asked by parents to address a child's change in gender identity, these tend to be quick conversations that focus on the child rather than on the construction and discussion of gender in the wider educational context (Ferfolja & Ullman, 2021). Teachers can assume that other parents will feel uncomfortable with teachers teaching gender diversity to their children. However, there is no evidence to suggest this is true (Ullman, Ferfolja & Hobby, 2021). Teachers' lack of knowledge here could be directly linked to teacher training, in that training in gender diversity has not always been easily accessible; optional workshops are the common method for most institutions (Fox, 2015). Therefore, teachers who exhibit little awareness of gender diversity end up being educated by the child themselves or their parents, which can cause distress for families (Davy & Cordoba, 2020).

Reflective activity

There are pros and cons to engaging parents as a conduit for pupil voice, as discussed earlier. There will also be specific pros and cons to this approach relevant to your educational context and the pupils you are thinking of working with. Use the boxes in Figure 7.2 to consider these in relation to pupils who may find it challenging to self-advocate. Reviewing the pros and cons you have listed, would you use this approach to enhance voice practices supporting pupils of diverse genders? Would it be appropriate to your setting?

Pros to using parents as a conduit for Pupil Voice	Cons to using parents as a conduit for Pupil Voice

Figure 7.2 Pros and cons of parents representing their children.

Teachers as allies

Some teachers become known as allies (meaning to be supportive) of gender diverse discourse. They hold important roles in involving gender diverse pupils' in participatory activities within the school, such as listening to them, validating their thoughts, and helping to create institutional change (Mannion, 2007). In this respect, children are provided with the opportunity to be consulted and informed in a respectful and understanding way, with the potential for institutional change (Hart, 1992). However, it has been found that most school allies have limited knowledge and experience to manage issues of gender diversity in schools, and those that did were found to be unreliable in listening to pupils (Meyer & Keenan, 2018). Furthermore, the use of the allied voices may mask the child's own voice (Meyer, 2016).

Reflective activity

Do you consider yourself an ally? How many other practitioners in your setting would consider themselves allies? What training is potentially required to strengthen allyship amongst staff?

Curriculum focus

One approach for creating a safe climate for voice practices for pupils of diverse genders is to enlist the help of a variety of visiting speakers who will act as social models for expressing voice (Naumann, 2018). This is an attempt to widen curriculum topics schoolchildren are exposed to. Bragg, Renold, Ringrose, and Jackson (2018) stated that a visiting speaker might lead children to feel uneasy at first, but that over time this would be something that children could get used to. However, an issue with visiting speakers is that this can further segregate gender diversity discussions away from the daily curriculum (Robinson, 2013).

A similar approach is student workshops that seek to include real voices, from real people, with real experiences to reduce the hostility felt by the school culture and increase student's supportiveness of each other (Burford, Lucassen, & Hamilton, 2017). However, although 80% of school members felt this was beneficial in reducing stigma, a similar issue arises where segregating these workshops away from the curriculum only further highlights gender difference more rather than creating emancipatory change (Burford et al., 2017). To create normalcy within schools, we must not focus exclusively on including the voices of pupils with diverse genders but to incorporate diverse gender perspectives in all aspects of school life (Stafford, 2016). To do this, schools need to know (from the perspectives of pupils) which areas of school life need to change.

Another way to diversify the curriculum is utilising gender diversity awareness children's books to bring about discussions within the classroom. Ryan, Patraw, and Bednar (2013) found that even young children were able to question complex societal ideas about gender and apply their thinking to develop ideas about what the school could do to incorporate more gender inclusivity. However, DePalma (2016) cautions the use of diversity awareness books because teachers might assume an identity of a character over an unsaid identity or where an identity is missing, such as assuming a "gay identity" over an unsaid transgender identity, which could be used for more in-depth critical discussions (DePalma, 2016, p. 829).

Teachers need to apply more fluidity in their own assumptions so that children's education is inclusive of all gender diversities (DePalma, 2016). To achieve more fluidity, diverse books could be used to propel children's thinking further by incorporating more creative educational and cross-curricular pursuits, such as using the books to create dramatisations, music renditions, and artistic drawings (DePalma, 2016). A further option to improve children's' participation could be to shift the process of teaching from the traditional adult-to-child approach towards a much more progressive child-to-teacher method. Children are much more aware of their world than teachers are and will have far more knowledge of gender diversity and equality than practitioners (Bragg et al., 2018).

Reflective activity

The following steps will guide you in engaging in curriculum activities that will enhance the voice of gender diverse pupils in your setting. They also direct you to consider designing a lesson that will allow pupils to teach you about their experiences and perceptions of gender diversity.

- Introduce pupils to gender diversity through the utilisation of gender diversity awareness literature.

- Discuss gender diversity openly in all its forms, for example, male, female, transgender, intersex, and agender.

- Provide pupils with the topic for a future lesson on gender diversity. This could be discussed with the pupils to add a further child-led element to this lesson.

- Let children know that they will be responsible for the teaching on that day or in that lesson, and that they can do their teaching in whichever way they choose. Examples of pedagogy, resources, or materials can be provided to the children, but reassure them that it is ultimately their choice.

- Provide the children with the time to research their ideas and help them to formulate their lesson plan.

- Finally, formulate and undertake a child-led lesson that is fully based on the children's ideas.

Gender voice groups

Encouraging gender diverse individuals to become involved in existing pupil voice representational systems should be cautioned. Robinson and Taylor (2007) said that privileged pupils often monopolise such systems as they possess the social "capital" to communicate effectively, due to understanding of the culture of the school (Bourdieu, 1977). This exclusion in pupil voice processes has resulted in schools ignoring full "democratic inclusivity" (Robinson & Taylor, 2007, p. 11). There will be students of some genders who will be more likely to be ignored than others just because of their identity (Fielding, 2004; Ruddock & Fielding, 2006). Improvements to this method could be achieved by removing any student hierarchical structures, such as removing any electoral processes that pupils must navigate before partaking in student representative systems (Quinn & Owen, 2016; Perry-Hazan, 2021).

An alternative could be achieved through the creation of student advocacy groups or student mentoring schemes where pupils can feel safe participating in feedback (Robinson & Taylor, 2007; Philipson, 2012; Perry-Hazan, 2021). One approach would be for all individuals in the school to come together to create what Stafford (2016, p. 11) calls "solidarity in action rather than focusing on 'difference.'" This requires the school to provide all children and all staff members with a duty to come together daily to support gender diversity and equality within schools (Stafford, 2016). In this method, children's voices would be constantly heard, constantly listened to, and will be constantly acted upon (Stafford, 2016). As such, any voice groups should encompass both target children whose voices you wish to highlight and allyship members.

Reflective activity

Use the tool in Figure 7.3 to plan a voice advocacy group for gender diversity in your educational setting.

Name of group:	Purpose / rationale:
GROUP MEMBERS	
Pupils whose voice I wish to advocate for:	Goals:
Pupil allyship:	Potential voice activities for group to engage with:
Staff allyship:	

Figure 7.3 Voice advocacy group. advocacy group.

Creative methods

A range of educational research studies have demonstrated that creative methods are an inclusive avenue for enhancing the voice of pupils with diverse genders. Mackenzie and Talbott (2018, p. 666), for instance, stated that creative methods enable children to demonstrate their lived experiences without the need for words, which would ultimately provide a much more inclusive approach to gender voice diversity than that experienced in other whole-school approaches, such as leaflet circulation. Creative methods for collecting voice have included utilising a multitude of activities, such as photo sharing, mapping, and "gender jars" (Bragg et al., 2018; Renold, 2018). These have enabled researchers to obtain the pupil voice regarding students' experiences of gender diversity in schools, bringing about discussions on gender boundaries, such as past conceptualisations of gender, through to the more contemporary interpretations of gender diversity (Bragg et al., 2018).

Creative methods move from "adult-initiated" activities towards completely "child-initiated" activities (Hart, 1992). To do this, practitioners such as yourself could discuss with the children in your classroom the many different methods in which human beings can communicate, such as verbal feedback, drawings, posters (see Stafford, 2016), photographs (see Mackenzie & Talbott, 2018), and mind-mapping (see Bragg et al., 2018). These will give you a range of activities to utilise.

Reflective activity

Photovoice is a research method that utilises the photos of participants as a creative way for exploring their views and perceptions on a topic. This strategy can be adapted and used as a tool in educational settings for promoting voice. Read the following summary of a photovoice project and then consider how this approach could be adapted and used in your setting.

Mackenzie and Talbott (2018) enabled pupils of all genders within a school to have a voice by utilising photovoice as a means of collecting their experiences of gender equality and diversity, as part of a whole-school community event. They found that the children were keen to explore their gender identities, stereotypes, and the exclusionary spaces within the school that were viewed as gender specific, such as by taking photographs of lavatories and play areas. Mackenzie and Talbott's photovoice approach was introduced by the adults in the school but was undertaken by children.

Ideas for how Photovoice could be used in my educational setting:

_____

_____

_____

_____

Figure 7.4 Photovoice ideas.

Chapter summary

How we culturally construct and understand gender is being challenged. As a result, educational settings are having to change in response to their pupils' diversifying gender presentations. New societal discourses are always challenging, and meaningful voice practices gain heightened importance. Children and young people are sharing new ways of conceptualising gender, and progressive ways of understanding and responding are emerging. One of these that has been presented in this chapter is a gender-creative approach, as it embodies a more reformist point of view. Whilst we are not advocating for revolutionary overhaul of your educational setting, we are seeking to provide challenge as a means for you to understand your own stance and develop your own meaningful voice practices for gender diverse pupils. As demonstrated in this chapter, there are many practical avenues that can be taken to achieve this, each with its own advantages and disadvantages. As this may well be new territory for you and your educational context, consider exploring feasibility projects and piloting before full-scale changes are actioned. This way you can always ensure you are staying close to the views and opinions of your gender diverse pupils.

Further reading

Sonja Mackenzie and Ashleigh Talbott, 2018, "Gender justice/gender through the eyes of children: A Photovoice project with elementary school gender expansive and LGBTQ-parented children and their allies," *Sex Education*, *18*(6), 655–671 – This research article provides the reader with an outline of photovoice being used as a research method for collecting voice from pupils with a diverse array of genders within schools. Although this research was used as part of a whole-school event, we hope that you will be able to see the value of implementing photovoice within the school culture and curriculum to influence change within your setting.

Anika Nicole Stafford, 2016, "'I feel like a girl inside': Possibilities for gender and sexual diversity in early primary school," *BC Studies: The British Columbian Quarterly*, *189*, 9–31 – This article discusses the challenges associated with hierarchical power relations and attempts to provide ideas for change that will promote the use of children's own agency within the setting. Therefore, we hope that you will be able to use this article as a resource to gain various educational ideas that you can use when undertaking gender equality and diversity within you setting.

Action plan

PLAN			
ETHOS What is your views on gender diversity in educational settings and how to you want to promote diversity and inclusion in relation to this?		**GOALS** What do you want to achieve?	
DO			
TASKS Break your goal into discrete tasks to be completed	**TIME LIMITS** Set a realistic time for your tasks to be completed by	**RESOURCES / ACTIONS / ACTIVITIES** What resources will you use? Who is responsible for doing what?	**COMPLETED** Tick this box when each task has been achieved.
REVIEW			
WHAT WENT WELL?	**WHAT WOULD YOU DO DIFFERENTLY?**	**WHAT ARE YOUR ONGOING PLANS FOR DEVELOPING PUPIL VOICE PRACTICES?**	

Figure 7.5 Supporting pupils of diverse genders action plan.

References

Ainsworth, C. (2015). Sex redefined. *Nature*, *518*(7539), 288–291.

Aultman, B. (2014). Cisgender. *TSQ: Transgender Studies Quarterly*, *1*(1–2), 61–62.

Barker, M., & Iantaffi, A. (2019). *Life isn't binary*. London: Jessica Kinsley Publishers.

Bem, L. S. (1981). Gender schema theory: A cognitive account of sex typing. *Psychological Review*, *88*(4), 354–364.

Bem, L. S. (1983). Gender schema theory and its implications for child development: Raising gender-aschematic children in a gender-schematic society. *Signs*, *8*(4), 598–616.

Blakemore, O. E. J., Berenbaum, A. S., & Liben, S. L. (2009). *Gender development*. East Sussex, UK: Psychology Press.

Bourdieu, P. (1977). Cultural reproduction and social reproduction. In J. Karabel & A. H. Halsey (Eds.), *Power and ideology in education* (pp. 487–511). Oxford: Oxford University Press.

Bragg, S., Renold, E., Ringrose, J., & Jackson, C. (2018). 'More than boy, girl, male, female': Exploring young people's views on gender diversity within and beyond school contexts. *Sex Education*, *18*(4), 420–434.

Burford, J., Lucassen, M. F. G., & Hamilton, T. (2017). Evaluating a gender diversity workshop to promote positive learning environments. *Journal of LGBT Youth*, *14*(2), 211–227.

Butler, J. (1988). Performative acts and gender constitution: An essay in phenomenology and feminist theory. *Theatre Journal*, *40*(4), 519–531.

Davies, B. (2003). *Frogs and snails and feminist tales*. Easthampton: Hampton Press.

Davy, Z., & Cordoba, S. (2020). School cultures and trans and gender-diverse children: Parents' perspectives. *Journal of GLBT Family Studies*, *16*(4), 349–367.

DePalma, R. (2016). Gay penguins, sissy ducklings … and beyond? Exploring gender and sexuality diversity through children's literature. *Discourse: Studies in the Cultural Politics of Education*, *37*(6), 828–845. https://doi.org/10.1080/01596306.2014.936712

Ehrensaft, D. (2011). *Gender born, gender made*. New York: The Experiment Publishing.

Erdol, T. A. (2019). Practicing gender pedagogy: The case of Egalia. *Eğitimde Nitel Araştırmalar Dergisi*, *7*(4), 1365–1385.

Ferfolja, T., & Ullman, J. (2021). Inclusive pedagogies for transgender and gender diverse children: Parents' perspectives on the limits of discourses of bullying and risk in schools. *Pedagogy, Culture & Society*, *29*(5), 793–810.

Fielding, M. (2004). Transformative approaches to student voice: Theoretical underpinnings, recalcitrant realities. *British Educational Research Journal*, *30*(2), 295–311. https://doi.org/10.1080/0141192042000195236

Fox, R. K. (2015). Is he a girl? Meeting the needs of children who are gender fluid. In. J. A. Sutterby (Eds.), *Discussions on sensitive issues*. West Yorkshire, UK: Emerald Group Publishing Limmited.

Hart, R. (1992). *Children's participation: From tokenism to citizenship*. UNICEF Innocenti Essay, no. 4. Florence, Italy: International Child Development Centre of UNICEF.

Josephidou, J., & Bolshaw, P. (2020). *Understanding gender and early childhood*. London: Routledge.

Kellett, M. (2010). Small shoes, big steps! Empowering children as active researchers. *American Journal of Community Psychology*, *46*(1–2), 195–203.

Kohlberg, L. (1966). A cognitive-development analysis of children's sex-role concepts and attitudes. In E. Maccoby (Ed.), *The development of sex differences*. Redwood City: Stanford University.

Mackenzie, S., & Talbott, A. (2018). Gender justice/gender through the eyes of children: A Photovoice project with elementary school gender expansive and LGBTQ-parented children and their allies. *Sex Education, 18*(6), 655–671.

Mannion, G. (2007). Going spatial, going relational: Why "listening to children" and children's participation needs reframing. *Discourse: Studies in the Cultural Politics of Education, 28*(3), 405–420.

Martin, C. L., Ruble, D. N., & Szkrybalo, J. (2002). Cognitive theories of early gender development. *Psychological Bulletin, 128*(6), 903–933.

Martin, K. A. (2005). William wants a doll. Can he have one? Feminists, childcare advisors, and gender-neutral child rearing. *Gender & Society, 19*(4), 456–479.

Meyer, D. (2016). The gentle neoliberalism of modern anti-bullying texts: Surveillance, intervention, and bystanders in contemporary bullying discourse. *Sexuality Research and Social Policy, 13*(4), 356–370.

Meyer, E. J., & Keenan, H. (2018). Can policies help schools affirm gender diversity? A policy archaeology of transgender-inclusive policies in California schools. *Gender and Education, 30*(6), 736–753.

Mischel, W. (1966). A social learning view of sex differences in behavior. In E. Maccoby (Ed.) *The development of sex differences*. Redwood City: Stanford University Press.

Morris, A. (2018). It's a Theyby. *New York Magazine*, 2 April, pp. 40–43.

Myers, K. (2020). *Raising them: Our adventure in gender creative parenting*. Seattle, WA: Topple Books.

Neumann, M. (2018). Gender and sexual diversity in international schools. *International Schools Journal, 38*(1), 52–58.

Pearson, R. (2021). Masculinity and emotionality in education: Critical reflections on discourses of boys' behaviour and mental health. *Educational Review*. Advance online publication.

Perry-Hazan, L. (2021). Conceptualising conflicts between student participation and other rights and interests. *Discourse: Studies in the Cultural Politics of Education, 42*(2), 184–198. https://doi.org/10.1080/01596306.2019.1599324

Philipson, J. M. (2012). Kids are not all right: Mandating peer mediation as a proactive anti-bullying measure in schools. *Cardozo Journal of Conflict Resolution, 14*, 81–104.

Quinn, S., & Owen, S. (2016). Digging deeper: Understanding the power of 'student voice'. *Australian Journal of Education, 60*(1), 60–72. https://doi.org/10.1177/0004944115626402

Renold, E. (2018). 'Feel what I feel': Making data with teen girls for creative activisms on how sexual violence matters. *Journal of Gender Studies, 27*(1), 37–55.

Reygan, F. (2019). Sexual and gender diversity in schools: Belonging, in/exclusion and the African child. *Perspectives in Education, 36*(2), 90–102.

Risman, B., & Myers, K. (1997). As the twig is bent: Children reared in feminist households. *Qualitative Sociology, 20*(2), 229–252.

Robinson, K. H. (2013). Building respectful relationships early: Educating children on gender variance and sexual diversity. A response to Damien Riggs. *Contemporary Issues in Early Childhood, 14*(1), 81–87.

Robinson, C., & Taylor, C. (2007). Theorizing student voice: Values and perspectives. *Improving Schools*, *10*(1), 5–17. https://doi.org/10.1177/1365480207073702

Ruddock, J., & Fielding, M. (2006). Student voice and the perils of popularity. *Educational Review*, *58*(2), 219–231. https://doi.org/10.1080/00131910600584207

Ryan, C. L., Patraw, J. M., & Bednar, M. (2013). Discussing princess boys and pregnant men: Teaching about gender diversity and transgender experiences within an elementary school curriculum. *Journal of LGBT Youth*, *10*(1–2), 83–105. https://doi.org/10.1080/19361653.2012.718540

Sandstrom, M., Steir, J., & Sandberg, A. (2013). Working with gender pedagogies at 14 Swedish preschools. *Journal of Early Childhood Research*, *11*, 123–321.

Short, S. E., Yang, Y. C., & Jenkins, T. M. (2013). Sex, gender, genetics, and health. *American Journal of Public Health*, *103*(Suppl 1), 93–101.

Stafford, A. N. (2016). "I feel like a girl inside": Possibilities for gender and sexual diversity in early primary school. *BC Studies: The British Columbian Quarterly*, *189*, 9–31.

Statham, J. (1986). *Daughters and sons: Experiences of non-sexist childraising*. Oxford: Basil Blackwell Ltd.

The Genderbread Person. (2022). Available at: https://www.genderbread.org/ [Retrieved: 13 March 2022].

The United Nations Convention on the Rights of the Child. (1989). Available at: https://www.unicef.org.uk/what-we-do/un-convention-child-rights/ [Retrieved: 3 November 2021].

Ullman, J., Ferfolja, T., & Hobby, L. (2021). Parents' perspectives on the inclusion of gender and sexuality diversity in K-12 schooling: Results from an Australian national study. *Sex Education*, 1–23.

West, C., & Zimmerman, H. D. (1991). Doing gender. In J. Lorber, & A. S. Farrell (Eds.). *The social construction of gender*. London: Sage.

Chapter 8

VOICE PRACTICES TO SUPPORT LGBTQIA+ EDUCATORS AND PUPILS

Alexandra Sewell, Max Davies, Jennifer Zwarthoed, Alexandra Baird, Klaudia Matasovska, Max Kirk, and Pippa Sterk

Introduction

This chapter will:

- Act as an appreciative space for the voices of LGBTQIA+ educators to be spoken and heard.

- Explore the implications of testimonial injustice in limiting the capacity of LGBTQIA+ educators, children, and young people as knowers and testifiers.

- Propose further challenges to voice practices in educational contexts.

The story of this chapter

The format of this final chapter is different from those that precede it. Originally, the chapter was planned as a discussion of voice work theories and practice examples for meaningfully listening and responding to LGBTQIA+ children and young people, with complementary workbook activities. I (Alexandra Sewell) sought a contributor to take editorial responsibility for the chapter. As with all contributors who took control of a chapter, I deemed it important that they were representational of the communities being written about. I also felt that I should approach colleagues and peers who I already had a working relationship with and respected their work. The rationale for this was that in producing a book about meaningful voice practices, I was not falling into tokenistic methods.

For practical reasons, this unfortunately did not come to fruition for this final chapter. The colleagues and peers I approached did not have the time to complete a chapter,

DOI: 10.4324/9781003165842-8

which is a real-world example of a pragmatic barrier to meaningful voice work that has been highlighted throughout this book. I still did not think it appropriate for me, with no lived experience of the topic, to take leadership in writing the chapter. This is where Max Davies, a contributor from Chapter 7, stepped forward. They had the creative idea of inviting a range of educational professionals who identify as LGBTQIA+ to share their perspectives. We kept the brief open to enable a wide range of views and experiences to hopefully be expressed. These are presented in this chapter and are further explored from the theoretical perspective of epistemic injustice, first introduced in Chapter 1. This final chapter ends with some further considerations for the future of meaningful voice practices in educational contexts.

The story of how this chapter came to be is shared here to demonstrate that meaningful voice work sometimes has to be adapted to evolving contexts. Whilst this book has presented many practice-based examples, do not feel that you should follow a step-by-step process when developing your own inclusive educational voice practice. As we have done here, if you hold your values close to you they can act as a path for appropriately canvassing the views and opinions of others, even when your initial plans are not feasibly possible.

LGBTQIA+ testimony and testimonial injustice

Our adapted resolution for this chapter is to share the testimony of educators with LGBTQIA+ experience. Testimony is a unique human experience; to speak our truth. Testimonial injustice occurs when what a person says is not believed by a hearer based on existing prejudices. It is a form of epistemic injustice (see Chapter 1) (Fricker, 2007). The credibility of a person is eroded, not because of the content of their speech, but because of a personal characteristic that is prejudiced. This leads to harm that has tangible consequences.

Firstly, the individual sharing their perspective is wronged as a knower (Burroughs & Tollefsen, 2016; Fricker, 2007). Part of the central experience of communicating is to have our own production of knowledge validated by others acting as responsible hearers, that is believing that we are a credible source. If this repeatedly doesn't happen, people come to question their own beliefs and mistrust their own perspectives (Burroughs & Tollefsen, 2016). This can have a secondary effect, especially prevalent in educational and learning contexts; the speaker's mistrust in their own views leads them to lack "intellectual self-confidence" (Burroughs & Tollefsen, 2016, p. 363). They begin not to speak out at all. The wider teaching and learning community is then harmed, as missed opportunities for developing collective knowledge occur. In educational contexts this limits both expression and discussion, two key ingredients in a dynamic learning environment.

Both LGBTQIA+ educators and pupils are subjected to this form of epistemic injustice (Beck, 2021; Fricker, 2007). Beck (2021) calls for the issue of testimonial injustice against LGBTQIA+ teachers to be raised to understand and respond to "oppression in teacher education programs by providing more nuanced ways to identify credibility deficits, to position teacher candidates as speakers, and to help teacher education faculty become better hearers" (p. 13). It is not enough to merely give space for LGBTQIA+ voices. The content of what they share needs to be taken as credible, especially pertaining to their unique lived experiences.

The following testimonies are from LGBTQIA+ educators who responded to our widened contributor call for this chapter. After each voice is shared, you are given the reflective space to explore where testimonial injustice has potentially been an experience for them and how this could be changed. This type of reflection is modelled for you with additional commentary on testimonial injustice.

Testimony 1

Jennifer Zwarthoed

As a sex educator I personally try to create a safe learning environment for all my students and anyone attending my lessons. Discussions about sex are, to this day, still considered taboo and vulgar (Brooke, 2006), especially when it comes to LGBTQIA+ issues. Therefore, many sex education resources are created with the least information possible. Additionally, the representation of LGBTQIA+ identities in media and teaching resources has long lacked adequate representativeness (McInroy & Craig, 2016). Representations in traditional media are commonly over-sexualised personalities and have unrealistic positive life development that suffer from a lack of inclusiveness (Meyer, 2009; Nelson & Barry, 2005). While materials can be labelled as inclusive if they briefly mention lesbian and gay relationships exist, they fail to incorporate LGBTQIA+ issues as a whole. Much of the curricula is based on biological deterministic information that is written from a heteronormative perspective.

To overcome this, lessons have to go beyond the curriculum and offer an understanding that lives, identities, and sexual attraction can be different from what is offered in lesson materials. As young people are emotionally dependent on social acceptance from their immediate surroundings (De Moor, Van der Graaff, Van Dijk, Meeus, & Branje, 2019), it is crucial to offer an inclusive environment within the one place they spend the majority of their waking hours – school. Researchers on LGBTQIA+ inclusive school policies have successfully reported a decline in bullying from both LGBTQIA+ students and their heterosexual, cisgendered peers (Proulx, Coulter, Egan, Matthews, & Mair, 2019; Russell & Fish, 2016). The presence and visibility of information and support on LGBTQIA+ issues in school subjects such as history, social sciences, and sex education, as well as the presence of student-led groups and activities, are strongly correlated with affirming interactions with a positive school climate and better student adjustment (Russell & Fish, 2016; Snapp, McGuire, Sinclair, Gabrion, & Russell, 2015).

As a member of the LGBTQIA+ community myself and teaching in a multinational secondary school environment, coming out to my classes was quite scary. However, for me it really became a way of connecting the curriculum to real-world examples. The students who were highly religious did not dare to ask any questions when we were talking about LGBTQIA+ issues within the curriculum. But knowing their teacher is part of the LGBTQIA+ community opened up their curiosity. Just like they understand that different people have different religions and that you can't choose the way you were born, they accept that people are different when it comes to sexuality, gender identity, expressions, and romantic involvement. To create an understanding that lives can be different and that books and videos do not always tell the full story can be hard, but if my 12- to 18-year-old students can understand it, then why not everyone else?

Reflective commentary

In this testimony Jennifer shares poignant examples of both wider epistemic injustice and specific testimonial injustice. Concerningly, they share how the topic of LGBTQIA+ sex education itself can be completely dismissed due to pre-existing prejudices of it being "taboo and vulgar." This full dismissal leaves no space for individual and collective narratives and perspectives from the LGBTQIA+ community in sex education learning contexts, as highlighted by the limited sharing of relevant information in current resources. As such, a whole perspective and knowledge existence is erased from the epistemic community.

This arguably reflects a wider epistemic injustice: the exclusion of a group from collective truth making practices. This, however, can lead to specific incidences of testimonial injustice. Jennifer demonstrates how negative stereotypes of LGBTQIA+ individuals being "over-sexualised" can lead to a dismissal of any input in sex education curriculum and resources. This is a specific case of testimonial injustice that, as Jennifer contests, leads to a privileging of the "heteronormative narrative" in curriculum development.

Reflective activity

Jennifer emphasises that to counteract the testimonial injustice outlined in their testimony educators must "go beyond the curriculum." What examples do they give? Use their examples to develop three strategies that could be incorporated into your educational context to reduce the chances of testimonial injustice occurring.

1. _____
   _____
   _____
   _____

2. _____
   _____
   _____
   _____

3. _____
   _____
   _____
   _____

Figure 8.1 Notes.

Testimony 2

Alexandra Baird

Within my first educational doctorate module I considered how I redefined my professional identity, having changed my career from secondary school teacher to university lecturer. This role change required me to first deconstruct my previous teacher identity before gaining an appreciation of the values of the new organisation and sector, whilst engaging with professional development opportunities to support the continued formation of a new professional identity. Analysing my own narrative of this experience allowed me to grasp the potential higher education offered, particularly the freedom to bring my "whole self" into work rather than compartmentalising a variety of identities. I noted how my own lesbian identity had complicated my previous teacher identity, requiring me to negotiate my identity alongside the heteronormativity of the schools in which I taught.

Volunteering as a governor of a local primary school, I became interested in the new statutory inclusion of lesbian, gay, bisexual, and transgender content within relationships and sex education (RSE). This encouraged me to step forward to support teachers to rewrite the school's RSE policy and oversee parental consultation and curriculum delivery. Working with teachers to enhance RSE's prominence, I realised I did not fully appreciate how primary teachers felt positioned to support the RSE policy and curriculum. I have analysed relevant policies and identify how primary teachers feel positioned through their own discourse. My research aims to appreciate how teachers feel positioned, and to work alongside them to create and teach an inclusive and effective RSE curriculum.

The case study school is a large co-educational community primary situated in Greater London, England, where I was previously a voluntary governor. The school has no religious affiliation but the majority of pupils are Muslim, with a high proportion of English as an additional language (EAL) learners and higher than the national average of pupils receiving free school meals (FSM). Participants included five (cisgendered heterosexual-identifying) women from the school who held a range of positions, roles, and experience, but had all previously taught RSE and were currently teaching in Key Stage 2. Participants were asked to reflect upon RSE and the school culture via semi-structured online interviews. RSE lessons and other subject lessons were observed by the researcher. Teachers' reflections of lessons were gathered after observation through an informal discussion. I attempted to "think with (queer) theory" to "plug" into the data, working "within and against interpretivism" to make new connectivities. This concluded that the school's curriculum, pedagogies, and strategies could and should extend further in order to truly be the LGBT-inclusive school which it already judged itself to be.

Reflective commentary

Alexandra's testimony reveals the pressures of having to manage the negative impact prejudice had in minimising their voice. The requirement to compartmentalise parts of their identity demonstrates the reality of their lived experience of being an outsider to the epistemic norms of the learning community they taught in. This constant management of identity presentation reflects Burroughs and Tollefsen's (2016) findings that when an individual is faced with repeated testimonial injustice, they adapt in ways that can have negative personal consequences. In this case, in not being able to bring their "whole self" to their role as an educator. As discussed at the start of this chapter, through repeated experiences like this, those who experience epistemic injustice come to question their own beliefs and knowledge, as their perspective is continually invalidated (Burroughs & Tollefsen, 2016). In this example, a personal attempt to counteract epistemic injustice is made through their educational doctorate assignments and research. This highlights the importance of diversity representation in wider knowledge production communities, such as the academy, and extends to all educational contexts.

Reflective activity

What can be done to empower LGBTQIA+ people to claim their voice in a wide range of educational contexts?

Testimony 3

Klaudia Matasovska

Prior to the start of my PhD studies at the Educational Department at Goldsmiths, I worked as a behaviour lead in a special educational needs and disabilities (SEND) school for the blind. Prejudice is a learnt behaviour, and one way for the stigma and fear to dissipate is to openly talk about inclusive education, including relationships and sex education (RSE). The other way to manage this issue is to train teachers on how to make LGBT RSE accessible to children and young people with SEND. I did feel there was some fear around this amongst my fellow SEND educators.

Therefore, a few years ago, I contacted a national LGBT charity to ask it to help my school run an LGBT inclusion programme to introduce the concept of LGBT to our learners and also teach them and the staff about LGBT inclusion, which was, at the time, a largely unusual thing for a SEND school to do. Once we started implementing this programme, we created Rainbow Clubs as part of this process, which I used to run with other colleagues, and it was a success. The students told us how much they appreciated having LGBT role models around them and the opportunity to speak openly about any LGBT+ concept. This experience enabled them to see that being themselves is more than OK. They engaged in writing poetry about having this "rainbow" opportunity. They openly thanked us for not viewing them as "childlike" or asexual with regard to disclosures concerning sexuality. They enjoyed having discussions about gender identities and used their chosen pronouns. They understood the importance of having unisex toilets and neutral-coloured uniforms in their school, and they had input into the school's policies with regard to LGBT inclusion. They would also liaison with the school's library staff about having access to Braille LGBT+-themed story books. There was no fear around any subject. The sessions were inspired by what the students needed to talk about, not by what we wanted them to talk about.

Since then, I have had the opportunity to inform other SEND school leaders about effective ways in which their teaching staff can support children and young people who identify as LGBT+. I have also been asked to give an interview about this experience for Twinkl SEND Digest to inform the SEND educational community of the benefits of this type of inclusive approach. In my view, most children have an open-minded perspective. I believe one of the best ways to support school children in their settings is to give them the message that everyone deserves to be valued. We should start with this message in early stages of schooling and having a truly inclusive curriculum is key in this process. Every young person deserves to see themselves, their family, and the full diversity of our world reflected in their curriculum, in the books they read, on worksheets, and in posters on the walls. This experience has also inspired me to start my PhD studies. My PhD thesis is going to be about LGBT+ inclusion with regard to pupils with SEND, especially non-verbal or partially verbal students. This is a largely under-researched area. I am hoping my research will impact on SEND settings' ethos and curriculum in such a way that they will be fully inclusive and representative of young disabled LGBT+ students, including their identities.

Reflective commentary

Klaudia's reflections demonstrate that testimonial injustice can occur when individuals are not believed or given an equal voice because of multiple prejudices held by others against them. We can think of LGBTQIA+ individuals with SEND as potentially experiencing a double disadvantage in their perspective being recognised and validated as their SEND status can lead to staff members having "fear" about such discussions. Testimonial injustice is at risk of occurring as individuals' gender identities and sexual orientations are ignored or discounted due to a paternalistic prejudice that pupils with SEND can't accurately know themselves or possess sexual preference. Yet pupils were grateful that they were not viewed as "childlike or asexual" just because they were attending a special needs school.

Reflective activity

Having read Klaudia's testimony and the reflective commentary, consider the pupils in your school who are taught RSE. Are there any children who may be viewed paternalistically, their gender identity or sexual orientation discouraged or dismissed due to prejudices held by staff against any personal characteristics they possess? Take some time to explore why these prejudices exist in this context. You can also use the prompts in Figure 8.2. What is the potential first step towards supporting staff to overcome these prejudices and accept the voice of all LGBTQIA+ pupils?

Testimony 4

Max Kirk

My undergraduate degree was in natural sciences, and I was out as trans for all that time. During the latter half of that degree, as part of a module about science in schools,

**Personal characteristic example:
Religion or belief**

Potential prejudicial views held about child /
young person:

Influence on accepting their views and
opinions on gender identity and
sexual orientation:

**Personal characteristic example:
Age**

Potential prejudicial views held about child /
young person:

Influence on accepting their views and
opinions on gender identity and
sexual orientation:

**Personal characteristic example:
Ethnicity**

Potential prejudicial views held about child/
young person:

Influence on accepting their views and
opinions on gender identity and
sexual orientation:

Figure 8.2 Influence of personal characteristics.

I had to do a ten-week placement in a local school. We were allocated to our schools by an administrator in another department who, unknown to me, had conversations with a few schools about me as a placement student. She had good intentions I'm sure, as she was aware of my anxiety about being in a school. But it happened without my knowledge, and I was singled out among my peers as different. It made me feel like a problem for this administrator, something she had to figure out. And it made me feel powerless.

The handling of this took me entirely by surprise, perhaps naively, but I'd spent two years at university where my gender barely even came up in my academic life. On reflection, this was perhaps less a sign that it was a non-issue, but more because my discipline was in STEM, and personal identity didn't really come into it. I had tutors who misgendered me, but it was all about the next problem, not about us (students) as people. It was a double-edge sword: my gender never came up, so I didn't feel othered, but also … it *never* came up, even when it was perhaps appropriate. I'm in social sciences now, and it's certainly different.

I spoke to my module leader about it, and she calmed my anxiety, both about the placement and the way mine was arranged, like I was something to be "handled." Thankfully, I trusted her implicitly; she'd been someone I felt comfortable around, and we had some really long chats about gender, academia, life. If I hadn't trusted her, I wouldn't have had the courage to say something, not in a department that didn't talk about the personal. She took efforts to make me feel like all my peers, to not highlight that I knew my school placement far ahead of my friends.

My advice to practitioners isn't anything that I consider groundbreaking, honestly. I'd highlight first that a small act of allyship can mean a phenomenal amount to a nervous student – a demonstrator with a pronoun badge as well as their name on their lab coat would have calmed the racing of my heart every week in labs, as the only one in the room with their pronouns displayed. Minimal effort, potentially huge reward.

Going beyond that though, the most important thing: *be proactive*. In an ideal world, my faculty would have known which schools would be appropriate to place trans students before their first openly trans student on the module asked. But we live in a real world and academics are incredibly busy. So, I suggest this: when you come to think about it (even if that is when it's urgently relevant), where you might foresee potential challenges, try to think about ideas for ways forward proactively. Be prepared. Then be open and honest with your students. Include them, involve them. Treat them like the adults they are, without putting the burden on them to find a solution alone.

Reflective activity

Now that you have read all four testimonies and the three reflective commentaries, the final reflective task for this chapter is to create your own reflective commentary for Max's testimony. How have they potentially experienced epistemic and testimonial injustice? They call for educators to "be proactive." How could this be achieved based on what you have learnt from reading their testimony here?

Diverse voices in educational practice: A future-orientated summary

The story of how this chapter diverged from the original plan led me to further consider the complexities of meaningful voice work in educational practice. The experience of attempting to offer a safe space for valid LGBTQIA+ representation, but not fully realising this vision, influenced the writing of this summary to explore these complexities. I have termed it a "future-oriented" summary, as the complexities presented here are by no means resolved. Voice work and voice practices in educational contexts are arguably a nascent phenomenon. Seminal theory and related policy developments first occurred in the mid- to late 20th century, for example Arnstein's (1969) influential ladder of citizen participation (Chapter 1) and the United Nations National Convention on the Rights of the Child (1989). As such, we can view educational voice work as having undergone a process of initial theoretical understanding and practice embedding in the early 21st century, with the next developmental phase being a collected discussion of arising complexities and future-oriented solutions. In this summary, I have chosen to focus on othering and the difficulties of responding meaningfully to conflicting perspectives.

Othering

"Othering" is a concept developed in disability studies and educational sociology disciplines to describe how subgroups are formed in society through identifying characteristics (Carroll, 2016). Othered groups are "out-groups," as selected prominent characteristics are positioned as being atypical to a perceived normative human presentation (Carroll, 2016). This is apparent in choice of the root word *other* in the concept; the in-group is favoured, and the out-group is other to this. They are constructed and known through difference to a perceived norm.

How othering is realised is complex and resultant of many layered actions. Discursive activities have received particular focus (Connor, Gabel, Gallagher, & Morton, 2008). How we talk about humans allows us to construct and reconstruct normative categories and out-groups to these. Structural inequalities have also been examined (Connor et al.,

2008). A social classification group is in part formed by the societal laws and rules (both formal and informal) that distinguish them and dictate their entitlements and manage their affairs. Writing this book has been a discursive activity, both in terms of the narratives and perspectives created through the writing and the conversations between the collaborators and me in shaping the form and direction. Engaging in this discursive activity led to the complexity of potentially engaging in othering activity, whether intentionally or unintentionally.

The formation of this chapter offers a pertinent example. When first proposing the book, chapters were formed around "type" of voice practices, leading to "types" and classifications of persons: children, SEND children, parents, professionals, the Global Ethnic Majority, gender, and LGBTQIA+. This seemed a practical way to ensure wide representation. It also offered a means for identifying diverse contributors, helping to protect the book from a narrow scope and perspective. However, the difficulty encountered with finding a representative contributor for this chapter threw into relief the limitations of this approach. In wishing to platform diverse voices across the book, there was arguably now too narrow a "type" for supporting this goal. Ironically, by attempting to be representative, the format for chapters had potentially become a discursive act that othered and reinforced socially constructed human difference. The difficulty encountered also highlighted the lack of diversity within my own work and social circles. As with many revelations that have come from writing this book, this is something I shall endeavour to continue to reflect and act on.

This complexity of meaningful voice work is also apparent in the implementation of voice practices in educational contexts. For example, any projects that aim to gain the perceptions of children with SEND create a new structure within the school, which in turn constructs and reinforces the othering of children with SEND as a subgroup. As with the writing of this book, searching for diverse perspectives via "type" can offer practical benefits, such as an easier organisation and audit of voice activities. However, this is a meagre benefit if existing social constructions and coexisting inequalities linked to them are reinforced.

As such, the role of othering in voice work in educational contexts is one that requires further, deeper examination. The development of meaningful voice practices will arguably only arise if educators take time to consider the role of classification by type and constructions of perceived social norms that voice practice activities may reinforce and/ or create. This reflection should, as always, go beyond the discursive and be applied to insightful action for the goal of *meaningful* voice work to be realised. The following reflective activity is presented to allow you to begin to comprehend creative ways that voice work activities can be engaged in without potentially engaging in othering.

Reflective activity

Revisit the action plan that you completed in Chapter 2 (pupil voice) and Chapter 5 (SEND pupil voice). Can you find a way to combine practical elements of collecting and understanding voice to develop a new procedure that would focus on pupil voice, inclusive of the voices of children with SEND without othering them? This may not be fully possible, but the aim is to move towards inclusive voice practices that are equipped for understanding a diverse range of perspectives and experiences.

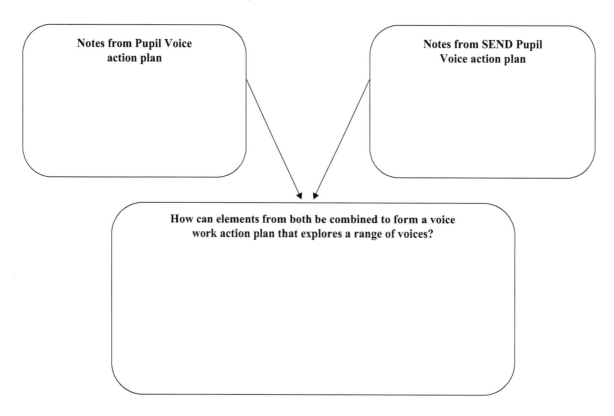

Figure 8.3 Joint action plan.

Othering: Case study

The following testimony is a demonstration of the lived experience of encountering "othering." Pippa Sterk attempted to align and integrate a student LGBTQIA+ support group in a higher education (HE) context with existing services, such as the counselling service. However, this was met with refusal and ignorance. By not responding openly to the requests, and being inclusive, existing social constructions and coexisting qualities were reinforced by HE staff.

(Content warning: The content of this case study includes references to and discussion of mental health and suicide.)

If we are hurting and nobody is there to hear us, do we still make a sound?

Pippa Sterk

When we consider LGBTQIA+ voices in education, our focus should not just be with the voice itself, the person expressing an opinion or a thought. It should also be on who is there to receive this voice, who can hear it, respond to it, channel it into something interpersonally meaningful. As LGBTQIA+ people in education, those who are there to receive our voices tend to be, more often than not, other LGBTQIA+ people. But what does it mean to only have each other to hear us?

When I was in my second year of my undergraduate degree, I joined my LGBTQIA+ student society's mental health peer support team. I wanted to lend an ear to people's worries and help fellow society members, many of whom had also become close friends. In discussing the logistics of the peer support group with the university's welfare team (undoubtedly underfunded and running on the goodwill of staff), we received very clear instructions: we were not to give people advice or tell them what to do. We could and should signpost people to "proper" support structures, to people who had actual training and expertise.

While I fully agree that a group of students in their late teens should not be giving *anyone* practical mental health advice, it was only after a couple of years outside of the university system that I began to question the way these interactions were heard institutionally. The peer support work was a response to what we, as LGBTQIA+ students, saw lacking in our educational environments: we saw our friends wait for months to be seen by a counsellor, only to then be met with outdated or even actively hostile attitudes towards gender and sexual non-conformity. We saw people drop out of degrees and disappear from university communities, seemingly without a sound. Yet this worry and distress inherent to the *need* for peer support was never addressed by the university.

On more than one occasion, we brought up to the university that we'd like to be trained to deal with serious issues like disclosures of sexual assault or suicidality, as these were topics that affected many people within the society. To my knowledge, nothing ever came of this request. The correspondence got lost (as so many things do at university) in a whirlwind of emails, handovers, changes of staff, and changes of students. However, institutional delay didn't mean that people weren't still suicidal and traumatised, just that there was nobody who knew how to help. We were doing what we could, but we knew we couldn't do much without potentially doing more harm than good.

The person who does the listening can affect what is being expressed. Our desire to set up a support group was parsed, institutionally, as a nice gesture from helpful students. A gesture of goodwill because you *want* to engage with other students in this way rather than because you know that if *you* don't take on this responsibility, there's a chance that nobody else will. In other ears, it could have been a scathing critique. A critique of a system that cares so little about the well-being of its students, they are forced to take care of each other without knowing how to.

Conflicting perspectives

We can think of the groups we designate for meaningful voice projects as voice communities. Despite the valid consideration that othering needs to be given, how to select and define a voice community will always involve a practical element of including and excluding individuals based on some form of marker. It is unrealistic to engage in a voice work project that will canvass the views of everyone. At the very least, context will delineate the group; for example, you may engage in a voice project in your school that seeks to canvass the collective views of all (staff, parents, pupils, etc.), but eventually your target group will fall within the context of the school itself. Otherwise, the task becomes nonsensical. Some of these ways of forming voice communities will be less subject to ethical concerns associated with discrimination. For example, delineating voice communities by year group or subject interest.

No matter along what lines a voice community is created, a secondary complexity is that of differing perspectives. There is often a tacit assumption in forming voice communities that whilst there may be some variations in opinions across individuals, these will only be slight differences of the same theme. This assumption itself can be viewed as a form of discursive othering; a simplification of the complexities of a perceived group. This view can obscure differing and conflicting views and opinions that are expressed within a voice community.

When the individual perspectives arising from a voice community dramatically differ from one another this can make the act of meaningfully responding very challenging. For example, I once worked with a group of individuals with SEND who offered different opinions on how I should physically make use of space in the classroom whilst teaching. Those with a hearing impairment shared that it was important for me to be visible and to mostly remain in one place to facilitate lip reading and use of assistive technology. Those with social and emotional needs reported that they liked it when I moved around a lot, and was sometimes close to them, as it kept their attention and helped them to feel confident to interact with me. These perspectives as to what type of teaching strategy would be inclusive were greatly at odds.

What should happen in such situations? I don't have a complete answer to this question. It may seem an odd choice to end a workbook like this, on an unresolved issue. However, with the challenges like this posed in each chapter, contributors and I have not sought to lead you, but to educate and provide opportunity for you to develop your own stance and related meaningful voice work practice. For this purpose, all activities have been *reflective* activities. This book has sought to challenge and guide rather than dictate and lead. It therefore seems apt to end on a similar challenge.

Future-oriented reflective activity

Revisit the conceptual statement for meaningful voice practice you developed at the end of Chapter 1. Rewrite it to include three future-oriented statements that acknowledge that your personal definition of meaningful voice practice is open to challenge and development.

Future-oriented statement
one:_____
_____
_____
_____

Future-oriented statement
two:_____
_____
_____
_____

Future-oriented statement
three:_____
_____
_____
_____

Figure 8.4 Future oriented statements.

Chapter summary

Meaningful voice practices in education are an exciting endeavour. They challenge us to consider who we wish to be as educators and how this can be enacted through our practice. Due to the personalised nature of meaningful voice practice, there is no template for this. In Chapter 1 you were assured that it is alright if your current voice practice does not yet align with your values and expectations. The purpose of this book has been to support you to clarify those values through reflection and to explore creative ways to pragmatically develop related actions. Just as who you are as an educator is in continual development, so too is your response to the views and perspectives of others you consequentially encounter. You will find many barriers and, as has been shown here, your original ideas will have to be adapted. Hold your values closely. Return to your own definition of meaningful voice practice. Use your moral code as a guide, be brave, and pursue worthy action that is inclusive of the diversity of voices in educational practice.

Action plan

PLAN			
ETHOS What is your orientation towards inclusive educational practice for LGBTQ+ pupils / staff?		**GOALS** What do you want to achieve?	
DO			
TASKS Break your goal into discrete tasks to be completed	**TIME LIMITS** Set a realistic time for your tasks to be completed by	**RESOURCES / ACTIONS / ACTIVITIES** What resources will you use? Who is responsible for doing what?	**COMPLETED** Tick this box when each task has been achieved.
REVIEW			
WHAT WENT WELL?	**WHAT WOULD YOU DO DIFFERENTLY?**	**WHAT ARE YOUR ONGOING PLANS FOR DEVELOPING PUPIL VOICE PRACTICES?**	

Figure 8.5 Supporting LGBTQIA+ pupils / staff action plan.

Further reading

Relationships and Sex Education 3–11: Supporting Children's Development and Well-Being by Richard Woolley and Sacha Mason – This book covers many perspectives on the topic of sexual orientation and attempts to foster the inclusion of children and young people's voice by offering strategies for developing pupil's questions about relationships and sex.

Sexual Orientation Equality in Schools: Teacher Advocacy and Action Research by Matthew Holt – This book includes the real stories of teachers seeking to tackle homophobia and heteronormativity in educational contexts.

References

Arnstein, S. R. (1969). A ladder of citizen participation. *Journal of the American Institute of Planners*, *35*(4), 216–224.

Beck, B. (2021). Testimonial injustice and teacher education. *Action in Teacher Education*, *44*(1), 1–17.

Brooke, S. (2006). Bodies, sexuality and the "modernization" of the British working classes, 1920s to 1960s. *International Labor and Working-Class History*, *69*, 104–122.

Burroughs, M. D., & Tollefsen, D. (2016). Learning to listen: Epistemic injustice and the child. *Episteme*, *13*(3), 359–377.

Carroll, M. (2016). Othering and its guises. *Philosophy, Psychiatry, & Psychology*, *23*(3), 253–256.

Connor, D. J., Gabel, S. L., Gallagher, D. J., & Morton, M. (2008). Disability studies and inclusive education: Implications for theory, research, and practice. *International Journal of Inclusive Education*, *12*(5–6), 441–457.

de Moor, E. L., Van der Graaff, J., Van Dijk, M. P. A., Meeus, W., & Branje, S. (2019). Stressful life events and identity development in early and mid-adolescence. *Journal of Adolescence*, *76*, 75–87.

Fricker, M. (2007). *Epistemic injustice: Power and the ethics of knowing*. Oxford: Oxford University Press.

McInroy, L. B., & Craig, S. L. (2016). Perspectives of LGBTQ emerging adults on the depiction and impact of LGBTQ media representation. *Journal of Youth Studies*, *20*(1), 32–46.

Meyer, M. D. E. (2009). "I'm just trying to find my way like most kids": Bisexuality, adolescence and the drama of *One Tree Hill*. *Sexuality & Culture*, *13*(4), 237–251.

Nelson, L. J., & Barry, C. M. (2005). Distinguishing features of emerging adulthood. *Journal of Adolescent Research*, *20*(2), 242–262.

Proulx, C. N., Coulter, R. W. S., Egan, J. E., Matthews, D. D., & Mair, C. (2019). Associations of lesbian, gay, bisexual, transgender, and questioning–inclusive sex education with mental health outcomes and school-based victimization in U.S. high school students. *Journal of Adolescent Health*, *64*(5), 608–614.

Russell, S. T., & Fish, J. N. (2016). Mental health in lesbian, gay, bisexual, and transgender (LGBT) youth. *Annual Review of Clinical Psychology*, *12*(1), 465–487.

Snapp, S. D., McGuire, J. K., Sinclair, K. O., Gabrion, K., & Russell, S. T. (2015). LGBTQ-inclusive curricula: Why supportive curricula matter. *Sex Education*, *15*(6), 580–596.

United Nations Convention on the Rights of the Child. (1989). Available at: https://www.unicef.org.uk/what-we-do/un-convention-child-rights/?sisearchengine=284&siproduct=Campaign_G_02_Our_Work&gclid=CjwKCAjwrNmWBhA4EiwAHbjEQPZ5TXH6-nVwH04aMtAAQXOQaSeHi8GbiOAKitlQ-A7TrveqPBpmexoCGfEQAvD_BwE [Retrieved: 3 November 2021].

INDEX